CAMBRIDGE

CAMBRIDGE

Tim Rawle

FRANCES LINCOLN • LONDON

Frontispiece:
The central colleges and the Backs.

Frances Lincoln Ltd

4 Torriano Mews

Torriano Avenue

London NW5 2RZ

www.franceslincoln.com

CAMBRIDGE

First Frances Lincoln edition 2005

A catalogue record for this book is available from the
British Library.

ISBN 0 7112 2549 4

Set in Gill Sans and Granjon and designed by Tim Rawle
Printed in China

9 8 7 6 5 4 3 2

The photographs in this book are all available as
high-quality prints at **www.cambridge-portfolio.co.uk**

CONTENTS

FOREWORD

I have always been fascinated by photography – as a schoolboy, through art school and architecture school, and as a designer and architect – but I was never trained as a photographer. At first the camera joined forces with my pencil and sketchbook, often as an aid to the bigger picture assisting with ideas, concepts and realisations, but it was not until later that it became an end in itself.

On foundation at St Martin's I thought I would be a painter or sculptor, but I soon realised the designer in me, and so moved to Central for graphics. It was there, under the influence of my tutor, Anthony Froshaug, that I picked up the architecture bug and sought change yet again. I was then fortunate to have the choice of either staying in London and going to the Bartlett School, trying something very different at Princeton in the United States, or going fifty miles north to that little market town on the edge of the East Anglian Fens with a reputation far bigger than itself. Wherever I might have gone a camera would have gone with me and I would have recorded my surroundings, with an inevitable bent towards the built environment. I just happen to have spent most of my adult life in Cambridge.

I remember arriving at Downing College in early October 1975, having left the buzz of London, and much else in my life, behind me, for a very different buzz in this very different place. I recall thinking what had I done. It all seemed very small, old, quiet, and a strange world after what I had been used to: the predominantly ancient architecture of the colleges; the narrow streets; the surprisingly modest Cam; male-dominated college life before mass co-education and in the dying days of old butlers and bulldogs, but still with gyps and bedders to look after your every need in the absence of Mum. This was an extraordinary little place of extraordinarily huge reputations – Marlowe, Milton, Pepys,

Newton, Wordsworth, Byron, Hardy, Brooke (that inexhaustible list) – but also, and far more comfortingly, Monty Python and Pink Floyd of not that long past. Perhaps it would not be so bad after all.

As an undergraduate in Cambridge you can lead a surprisingly sheltered existence centred around your college and university department, often not venturing far beyond for the three year 'internment', hence the age-old division of 'Town' and 'Gown'. Cambridge is a compact place, with much concentrated into its middle that has evolved over almost a thousand years. The buildings and the spaces around them – many of which are tracts from the countryside penetrating right into the nucleus as testimony to an enduring policy of conservation – make up this internationally famous little English city that so many have loved and adored, having spent, or misspent, the final years of their youth there. As Rupert Brooke so fondly recalled in a letter he wrote from Toronto to a friend in 1913:

My heart is sick for several things, only to be found in King's… I do recall those haunts with tears, the Backs, the Chapel, and the Rears… O places of perpetual mire, localities of my desire, O lovely, O remembered gloom… Haunts where I drank the whole damn night! Place where I catted till the light! Dear spot where I was taken short. O Bodley's Court! O Bodley's Court!

It has always seemed strange to me that I never got to know this place well until I had finished being a student, until I began really living here, rather than simply 'abiding', as Wordsworth put it, in his case, in his 'nook obscure' at St John's.

After this broad sampling of the arts, and seven continuous years a student, I found myself back in London working as an assistant architect, in the pre-CAD revolution days, drawing sections through foundations and roofs for buildings in the Arabian Gulf that I would never see. This was enough reality to dampen the excitement of any young architect, though a brief spell in the local Cambridge office of RMJM provided a glimpse of the satisfaction from drawing board to building site under the guidance of Buffery, Annand and Mustoe. Determination temporarily prevailed with postgraduate study at the Architectural Association, but I knew that the rigours and frustrations of architectural practice were not for me, though a love for buildings, old and new, has always remained.

After leaving practice I was lucky to be able to combine graphic design, architecture and photography with the production of two books, which made me concentrate on what I was doing with the camera and how the photographer looks at and approaches buildings, from both outside and in. It was at the suggestion and with the support of two observant local architects – John Cound and David Page – that my first book *Cambridge Architecture* came about, and this made me explore the city in more depth than I had ever done before. A few years later the Fellowship of Downing gave me the opportunity to oversee the production of *Committed to Classicism: The Building of Downing College, Cambridge*, working with Dr Cinzia Sicca.

Cambridge is an ongoing phenomenon and, like Oxford, has always changed with the times and taken advantage of its position to represent the *Zeitgeist* in every way, not only in things cerebral but in the built environment too, with many of the great English architects and most building styles being represented. There is a rich architectural heritage here, brought about by the wealth of the university and, more so, by the individuals who founded the thirty or so colleges –

kings and queens, aristocrats and noblemen, bishops, suffragettes and even a local lad made good from bicycle sales and television rentals. This richly layered fabric, coupled with the life and traditions that make the place breathe, have long intrigued me.

Half of the pictures in this book are the result of that now slowly waning technology – celluloid coated with chemicals – and old habits indeed die hard. Although my film camera still occupies a place in my bag – sadly, more of honour these days than necessity – the joys and amazing genius of digital technology have very recently taken me over. The Macintosh computer and stunning software have now become the photographer's darkroom, and the single pixel has transformed image production and manipulation into something quite extraordinary, the limits of which seem boundless. This book is my first major publication in which I have included a large number of digital pictures, and I shall leave it up to the discerning eye of the purist observer to decide which ones they are.

The book is a combination of an essay and a collection of photographs, some taken especially to illustrate the essay, others not. The aim of the text is to give a brief outline of how Cambridge has evolved and how it is currently experiencing major rejuvenation and expansion that will transform it into quite a different city in the near future. The photographs are simply a collection of pictures illustrating the richness of this place at a brief moment in its long history.

Tim Rawle, October 2005

ACKNOWLEDGMENTS

This all began a few days before Christmas in 1974, on a cold, wet evening in the senior tutor's rooms at Downing, when Mr John Hopkins and the late Peter Bicknell – a lawyer and an architect – offered me a place to start the following autumn. Without the enthusiasm of John Hopkins my life would have probably taken quite a different route.

This book has come about at the suggestion of a number of people over a number years, though much of the material here contained was never created for that end purpose, many of the images having been taken over the last few decades at random and with plenty of time to indulge the photographer's fussiness. The final impetus to turn this collection into a bound volume of pictures accompanied by a few words came out of many inspirational discussions with a friend who publishes and lives art books, and whose endless encouragement has now finally seen fruition – John Adamson. I am indebted to him for his invaluable help and guidance throughout this project.

Another essential person has been Matt Savage, who has helped me with the pre-press production of this book. To him I owe much for his technical expertise and admirable creativity in various software programmes and in all things digital. I would also like to thank James Shurmer, a designer and typographer of the old school now well versed in CAD, for advice and guidance; Mike Edwards for the conventional artwork in the distant past to create the college shields, and Graham Johnson for his work on the map and plan.

Two other photographers have made major contributions to pictures in this book. My old friend, Paul Smith, worked with me on difficult interiors at Trinity and King's (figs 84, 140), in the latter of which we 'painted' with light; and I combined forces and equipment with James Austen for the large interiors at King's and St John's (figs 41, 43–6, 139).

I am indebted to the generosity of the Fellowships of all the Cambridge colleges in allowing photographs to be taken of their beautiful buildings and sites, in particular: to King's for whom I have worked over many years; to Christ's for the recent pictures of the quincentenary celebration (figs 71–2), and most recently to the kindness of Professor and Mrs Ingram for allowing me access to the Master's Lodge at St Catharine's to photograph the otherwise very confined front of Queens' College (figs 54, 158). I am also grateful to the general staff of the colleges, especially to the porters and gardeners who do such a great job.

My thanks go to Sam Robinson, my former assistant, for his considerable endurance on a variety of tasks, and for a quick eye one snowy winter's day at Trinity, when in the path of a driving, disgruntled octogenarian don who tried to run down my tripod and Nikon, and possibly myself; to James and Rod at the Cambridge Punting Company for many mutually beneficial punting sessions on the Backs and the Upper River; and to Brian Human at the city planning department.

There are far too many other individuals to list here who, over the years, have helped, assisted or simply put up with the imposition of a photographer's needs, to all of whom I am most grateful for the results achieved. Of those, I would like to thank the helicopter pilots who took me up over Cambridge on several occasions and agreed to leave the passenger door of the little Robinson two-seater on the ground, ensuring that I was well strapped in but could lean out far enough to achieve the views desired – an enthralling experience.

For Ali, Katie, Ed, Jamie and Ellie.

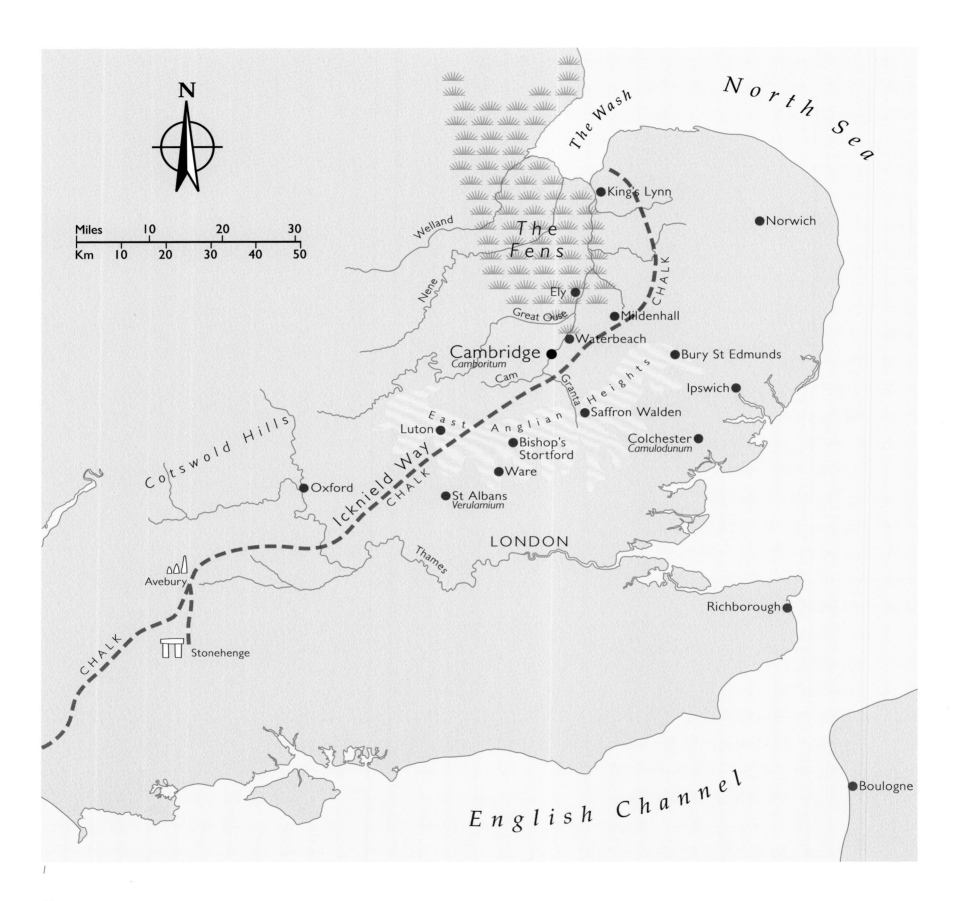

N

Miles   10   20   30
Km   10   20   30   40   50

North Sea

The Wash

King's Lynn

Norwich

The Fens

Welland

Nene

Ely

Great Ouse

Mildenhall

CHALK

Waterbeach

Bury St Edmunds

Cambridge
Camboritum

Cam

Granta

Heights

Ipswich

East   Anglian

Saffron Walden

Cotswold Hills

Luton

Bishop's
Stortford

Colchester
Camulodunum

Icknield Way

CHALK

Ware

Oxford

St Albans
Verulamium

LONDON

Thames

Avebury

Richborough

CHALK

Stonehenge

Boulogne

English Channel

CAMBRIDGE

Origins

When Julius Caesar invaded Britain from newly conquered Gaul some fifty-five years before the birth of Jesus Christ, his forces clashed with those of King Cassivellaunus and the dominant Catuvellauni tribe, who ruled the south-east from their capital at Verulamium near what is now St Albans. But Caesar's raids were not followed through and fierce opposition from the ancient Britons gave temporary respite from the expanding Roman empire at that time. A century later, around the end of the rule of King Cunobelinus – Shakespeare's Cymbeline – a more formidable Roman force of the great Emperor Claudius set sail from Boulogne in the summer of AD 43, landed unopposed at Richborough in Kent, and proceeded to finish the job. They forded the Thames and, headed by Claudius himself, marched triumphantly to take the new capital at Camulodunum in Essex, present day Colchester, only 40 miles to the south-east of Cambridge. It was at Camulodunum, a few decades later, that Queen Boudica (Boadicea) of the Iceni tribe, gave the Romans such a grand fight before total submission finally ensued. Once the Romans were established in Camulodunum, two legions headed northwards, and it is thought that it was the 9th Legion that set up a camp at

'Camboritum'. It is not clear how important this base was, but a few centuries later Bede tells us that the 'city' of Camboritum had walls of masonry and so it must have been of considerable significance as an ordinary camp would only have been protected by earthen ramparts. Bede's documentary evidence was borne out by portions of Roman brick walls that were found in the Castle Hill area of north Cambridge during early nineteenth-century excavations, and numerous archaeological finds there since have indicated a major settlement. The invading Roman forces gave considerable importance to this place at the crossing of the river, as did subsequent barbarian raiders throughout the Dark Ages long after the Romans had left. That importance was due to its location as the northernmost point before treacherous marshlands, with its defensible river crossing providing a gateway to the north or south-east.

Cambridge lies within the river system of the Great Ouse, which rises north of Oxford in the Cotswold Hills about 60 miles to the south-west, and enters the North Sea at King's Lynn on the Wash, about 40 miles to the north-east (fig. 1). To the immediate north of Cambridge lie the Fens, the extensive alluvial flood plains of the Ouse and the rivers

1. Diagrammatic map of south-east England showing the Cambridge area.

Nene and Welland, forming a large area of reclaimed marsh-land that is contained by a harder and higher belt of chalk to the east and south-west, on the edge of which sits Cambridge. Two rivers, both tributaries of the Ouse, converge just south of the city near the village of Trumpington: the Cam, which rises at Ashwell in Hertfordshire, and the Granta, which rises near Saffron Walden in Essex. They flow united through the city as the Cam to join the Ouse about 15 miles north near Ely. It is these two rivers – the Cam and the Granta – that have dictated the different names by which the city has been known throughout its history, depending on the river name chosen by the successive occupiers of 'the place at the crossing of the river': Camboritum (Roman), Grantacaestir (Anglo-Saxon, the name later adopted for the village of Grantchester, just south of Cambridge), Grantabrycge (Anglo-Danish), Cantebrig (Norman), and Cambridge thereafter, a name which was commonly used only from about 1600. When the name Grantabrycge appeared in the *Anglo-Saxon Chronicle* entry of 875, it may have been one of the earliest instances of the word 'bridge' in written English. It is also thought that the bridge over the Cam built by the Anglo-Saxon King Offa (757–96) may have been the first bridge of any importance to have been constructed in England after the departure of the Romans in the early fifth century. Today there are nine bridges across the river within Cambridge city centre, but only two of them are public road bridges: Magdalene Bridge in the north (next to Magdalene College), and the Silver Street Bridge in the south. Magdalene Bridge is on the site of the original Cam bridge. Before a bridge was built there would have been a ford across the river. In the mid-eighteenth century the local architect James Essex came across remnants of one when he was building a new stone bridge at the main crossing (the predecessor of the current iron structure) and noted that the ford 'very plainly shewed

itself as a firm pavement of pebbles'. It is interesting that unlike its age-old academic rival Oxford – at the place where oxen forded the river – the name 'Camford' did not evolve.

Primeval settlers were drawn to the Cambridge area by the river with its fertile valleys and surrounding high ground. In prehistoric times packmen and tribesmen would have passed through the area regularly as it was in the vicinity of the ancient Icknield Way, a major route that followed the high chalk outcrop which stretched all the way from north Norfolk to the West Country. Most of England at that time was covered in dense forest and undergrowth, and these chalk downs provided relatively clear tracts of high ground, affording unencumbered access to such centres of worship as Avebury and Stonehenge in Wiltshire. This combination of land routes, a navigable waterway, the river crossing and surrounding high ground led to the place acquiring strategic and military importance, firstly to the Romans, and then later to other occupying forces right up to William the Conqueror, who took it on returning from York in 1068, over a thousand years after the 9th Legion first made camp there. There is no visible trace of the Roman occupation at Cambridge, though two of their important roads did pass through the city: Akeman Street and the Via Devana. The Via Devana forms the main axis of the city as Hills Road to the south and the Huntingdon Road to the north (the current A604).

The geography of the Cambridge area was a crucial factor in those early days, shaping its development and prolonging its isolation and lack of accessibility to and from London until modern times. The area of high ground to the south known as the East Anglian Heights, stretching from Luton in the west to Bury St Edmunds in the east, the dense forest and heavy clay soil on the north side of the heights, and the equally hazardous Essex Forest to the east, made direct access very difficult. As a result, the journey between

London and Cambridge was a long and roundabout one, and this is why there is no 'London Road' in Cambridge, as there is in so many other English towns. It is not until 1655 that reference is made to a regular stagecoach service between London and Cambridge, carrying passengers and mail. The famous seventeenth-century diarist Samuel Pepys (1633–1703) records making many journeys between the two places, both by coach and on horseback, and it was either a pleasurable event taking two days and visiting his favourite inns *en route*, or a very long and arduous day from 4am to 8pm. It is now well under an hour by train into King's Cross.

The topography in Cambridge itself in these early days dictated settlement points on the few hilly outcrops rising above the flood plain of the river. On the west bank a gravel-capped outcrop of the chalk ridge provided a suitable escarpment for habitation that soon became the military vantage point from which the river crossing could be controlled, subsequently named Castle Hill. On the opposite, east bank of the river were three lower hills – Peas Hill, Market Hill and St Andrew's Hill – all of which remain today but are hardly discernible as hillocks. All along the banks, flanking the river on both sides from what is now Magdalene Bridge right down to the Mill Pool at Silver Street Bridge, was a wide area of marshy ground anciently known as 'The Thousand Willows'. That area was gradually reclaimed and artificially raised to form building land and is now occupied down its entire length by the central nucleus of colleges and their beautiful gardens known famously as the Cambridge Backs (fig. 2).

2. The Cambridge Backs – the area along the river in central Cambridge flanked on either side by gardens of several of the older colleges. This scene shows Clare College Bridge – the oldest surviving bridge across the river (1638–42) – in the early hours of a summer morning at the end of the college May Ball with party-goers being punted up-river for breakfast at Grantchester.

2

3. The river at Trinity and St John's Colleges, with the tower of St John's Chapel in the distance. Anciently known as 'The Thousand Willows', this area still has many fine trees, weeping willows in abundance, as seen here and in the pictures overleaf.

3

4 (left). Punting through the willows along the Backs towards Garret Hostel Bridge at the rear of Trinity Hall.

5. View through blossom towards the Bridge of Sighs from the Master's Garden at St John's College.

5

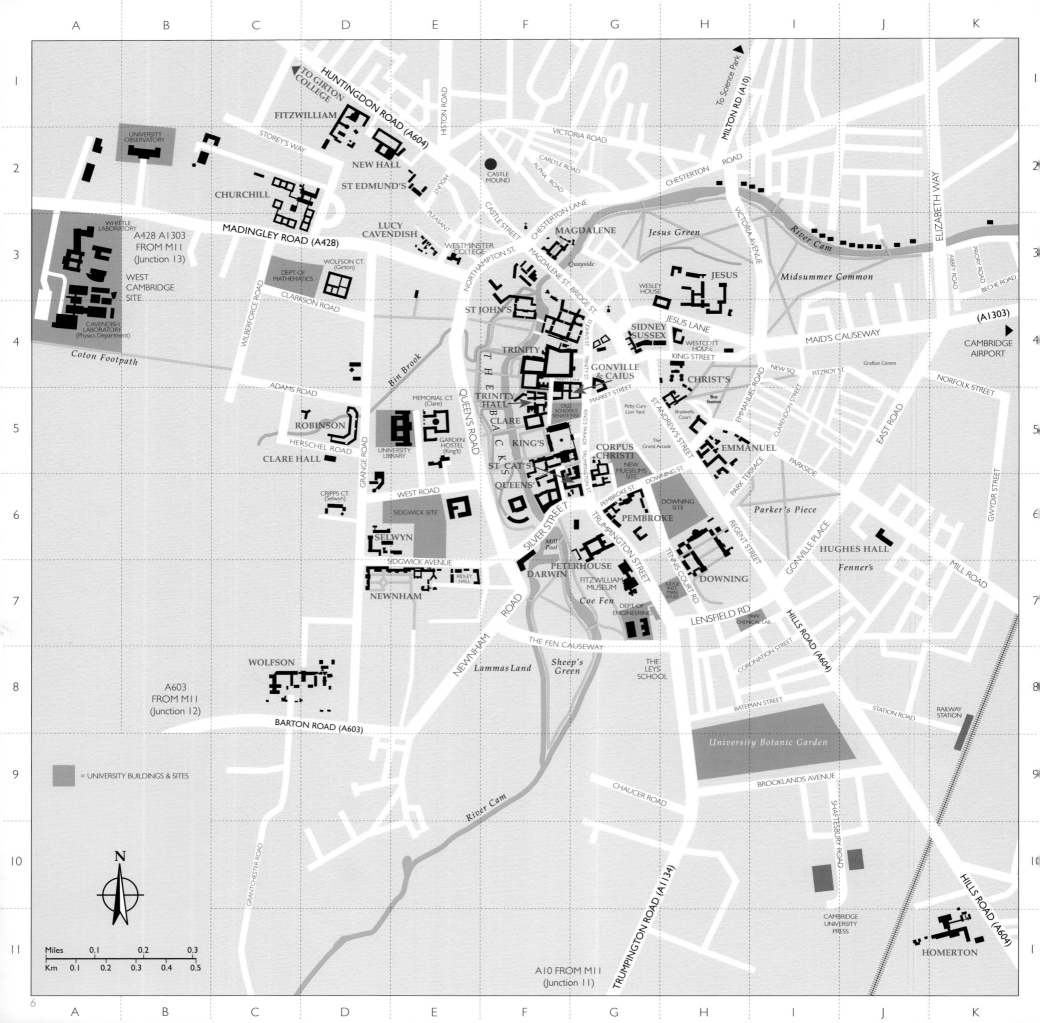

The present form of the city centre (fig. 6) developed in response to this early problem of acquiring suitable land on which to build, and it is now an extraordinary picture to imagine that large area of present-day Cambridge – from Castle Hill in the north, to the Fen Causeway in the south – as a collection of small settlements separated by marshy bogs and the river. From these primitive beginnings over a millennium ago it is possible to visualise how two Cambridges developed: one on each side of the river. For centuries feuding tribes then fought for control of the river crossing and in turn occupied either the dominating Castle Hill settlement or the less advantaged, lower marshy quarters. Anglo-Saxon Cambridge suffered much as it found itself between the two rival kingdoms of Mercia and East Anglia and it became, in effect, a battleground as the two tribes fought continually for control of the river crossing for many years. The Mercians were generally the stronger force as shown, for instance, by King Penda's destruction of the Castle Hill settlement after his victory over the East Angles in 634, and King Offa's control of the area throughout the second half of the eighth century, when he is credited with building the first bridge.

Northern Invaders

Feuding between the Mercians and the East Angles went on for about 250 years until c. 850, when the threat of the Vikings united most of the English kingdoms to defend the coastlines. East Anglia was particularly vulnerable to attack, and the Norsemen and Danes soon penetrated the region by sailing up its many rivers into the interior. The Great Ouse was just such an artery for Viking infiltration, and the Cam was a tidal waterway as far inland as Waterbeach, only 6 miles to the north, and from there the river was still a deep navigable channel up which Viking longboats could easily reach the city. From 865 until 869 a great Viking army ravaged the area continuously, and the *Anglo-Saxon Chronicle* records that in 875 Danes wintered at Cambridge. Three years later, under the Treaty of Wedmore, the area passed into the Danelaw, as did the whole eastern side of England from Teesside to the Thames.

The effect of the Danish occupation on Cambridge was very important as the Danes formed a major inland port at this convergence of land routes and waterway. By establishing their settlement next to the river, in what is now the Quayside area around Bridge Street and St Clement's Church (St Clement is a patron saint of sailors), they fused the two communities into one. Moreover, they brought unprecedented importance to the east bank of the river where they built the port itself, constructing numerous wharves and hythes. The port soon became the regional centre for trade and the town flourished greatly as a result for several centuries. Danelaw continued into the early tenth century until the Saxons, under Edward the Elder, King of Wessex, recovered the region in c.921. Edward then passed a law which stated that all trading must take place in a market town under the supervision of the justices, thus aiding the concentration of commerce in the new centres such as Cambridge.

The Danes laid the foundations of the English borough and its towns, and they introduced the division of the country into shires or counties, some of which were later named after their principal towns, as with Cambridge and Cambridgeshire. From this time onwards Cambridge was firmly established as the main county town, with Ely its religious centre. However, Edward failed to put an end to continuing Viking raids and many took place throughout the tenth and eleventh centuries, with the most fierce at Cambridge resulting in the burning of the town in 1010 just

6. *Diagrammatic plan of Cambridge city centre showing the principal collegiate and university buildings and sites.*

7. *The 'Wren' Bridge at St John's College, also known as the Old Bridge or Kitchen Bridge. Both Sir Christopher Wren and his collaborator, Nicholas Hawksmoor, were consulted about the design of this bridge, but neither had anything to do with its actual execution, though the name has remained over the years. It was built by a local mason, Robert Grumbold, in 1709–12.*

7

8. *The lower river along Midsummer Common.*

9. *The river, just below Jesus Green Lock.*

10. *A Jesus College Ladies Eight at the May Bumps, the annual summer collegiate boat races, taking a victory row back along the course with the cox holding the college flag.*

11. *Evening scullers on the Lower River turning at the end of the Long Reach, in the meadows at the village of Fen Ditton on the east side of Cambridge. The pinnacles of King's College Chapel with the tower of Great St Mary's Church, and the spire of All Saints Church, can be seen in the distance.*

10

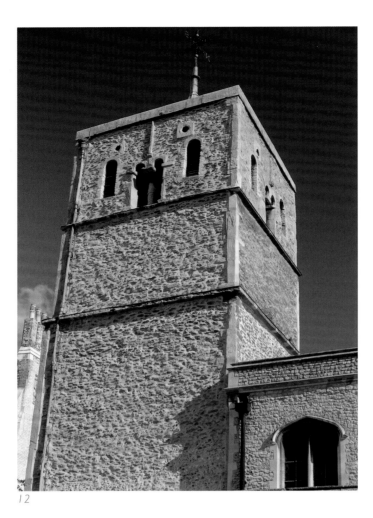

12. St Bene't's Church, the oldest surviving building in Cambridge. The pre-Conquest tower, and parts of the nave and chancel, were built in c.1040. Constructed in three successive, tapering stages, the upper section of the tower contains the belfry and is the most authentic, though the round-headed twin openings were added in 1586. The church was bought by the two town guilds of Corpus Christi and St Mary in 1350, and when they established their college in 1352 it served both the college and the parish until 1579 when the college built its own chapel. Major additions and restoration took place in the nineteenth century.

13. The oldest surviving house in the county, known as 'The School of Pythagoras' (c.1200), located in the grounds of St John's College.

12

13

prior to the last conquest by King Cnut (Canute). The Danes soon restored peace and organisation, and a town of such importance as Cambridge would have been quickly rebuilt.

Danish ingenuity in trading, combined with the Saxon market law of King Edward (who also established a royal mint at Cambridge), brought great prosperity to the town. The architecture at this time would have consisted of a collection of timber-framed buildings with thatched roofs and walls of cob or wattle and daub, all perishable materials of which nothing has survived. Archaeological evidence has suggested that there were two major structures at that time in the Castle Hill area: possibly the original church of Cambridge and a fortress guarding the river crossing. The new prosperity soon started to see the construction of the first stone buildings in the town, parts of which have survived to the present day: the tower of St Bene't's Church (fig. 12), along with smaller details in various other early churches, since largely rebuilt. Around the year 1200 the first stone house was built, the earliest surviving in the county – the so-called 'School of Pythagoras' (fig. 13), now in the grounds of St John's College. But only wealthy foundations or individuals could afford to build in stone, which had to be imported from elsewhere as there is no good building stone in the Cambridge area. The only local stone was a soft limestone known as 'clunch', which lends itself marvellously to carving but is not a substantial structural material. The nearest supply of good stone is to the north-west in Northamptonshire, where limestone quarries, such as that at Ketton, have been the source of many fine Cambridge buildings. Because of this lack of local stone Cambridge turned to brick making at an early date using the abundant clays to be found throughout the county, and this resulted in one of the most noticeable differences between it and Oxford: a large number of Cambridge buildings are of brick, whereas at Oxford, which is situated in an area rich in limestone, they are predominantly of stone. The impression one gets in Cambridge is, however, quite deceptive, as there do seem to be a lot of stone buildings, but this is due to a bit of cheating and there are far more brick buildings than it actually appears. During the Classical Revival of the seventeenth and eighteenth centuries, when the impact of the Italian Renaissance was at its peak, Gothic brick buildings became unfashionable and several of the colleges embarked upon a vast cosmetic operation to face many of their buildings with stone, especially those fronting the public streets (see p. 76).

Norman Cambridge

After the Battle of Hastings, William the Conqueror subdued Middle England in 1067–9 and established castles at Lincoln, Huntingdon and Cambridge, buildings that were symbols and instruments of Norman domination. Like his predecessors, William recognised the military importance of the settlement on the edge of the Fens, and the castle at his Cambridge was, of course, built on the high ground overlooking the river crossing, once again focussing attention on the west bank of the river. That castle did not survive, but it was an earthwork of the motte-and-bailey type, consisting of one or more fortified enclosures (baileys) dominated by a steep-sided earth mound with a flat top (the motte) on which stood the tower (the keep) normally built of stone, the whole structure being surrounded by ditches, banks or palisades. The surviving castle mound (fig. 14) shows that the motte was quite substantial, about 40 feet high by about 200 feet across.

The Norman Conquest instigated a swing away from the influence of northern Europe towards the mainstream of western European culture. In terms of architecture this was most important as the Normans brought with them an advanced building form in the Romanesque style, later to develop into the three phases of English Gothic. Once the Normans were established at Cambridge, substantial buildings of stone gradually began to appear. The castle had been built by William's Sheriff, Picot, and his wife, Hugolina, was later responsible for the first St Giles' Church on Castle Hill (since rebuilt) and a house of Regular Canons in 1092. The next Sheriff, the crusading knight Pain Peverell, enlarged that foundation and moved it to the more spacious setting in the fields on the eastern side of the town where it became known as Barnwell Priory. Little remains of the priory, except for a small chapel, now the parish church of St Andrew the Less on the Newmarket Road, and part of the kitchens, preserved in good condition on the corner of Priory and Beche Roads. In the mid-twelfth century several other monastic foundations arose. These were the Benedictine Nunnery of St Radegund (now part of Jesus College) and two hospitals administered by monks: the

14. The remaining motte of the castle, built by William the Conqueror in 1068. The castle was greatly enlarged by Edward I in 1283–1307 when he added a gatehouse with a barbican across the moat, angle towers and a great hall and chapel. Throughout the fifteenth and sixteenth centuries much of the stone was taken and used for new college buildings. By the early seventeenth century the only building left was the gatehouse, which survived until 1840. It was from this high vantage point that the river crossing was controlled by the Romans and then by feuding tribes throughout the Dark Ages.

14

15

16

15–17. The 'Wren' Bridge, St John's College (right), with sculpture bays from the bridge depicting watery scenes (left): Old Father Cam (top), with book in hand and the bridge and college behind, and Neptune (below).

19

18 (left). *Stylish craft at the May Bumps.*

19. *The 'Survivors' of Trinity College May Ball at 6 am. An uncharacteristically hot, early June dawn found these revellers having their picture taken by a local photographer who was hoisted up on a crane on the opposite bank.*

leper hospital beyond Barnwell, of which the perfect little Chapel of St Mary Magdalene has survived (fig. 20), and the Hospital of St John in the town centre, of which nothing remains, although this foundation was perpetuated as St John's College, one of the largest and most grand in Cambridge. The most spectacular Norman building to survive in Cambridge is the Round Church of the Holy Sepulchre, also in the town centre (figs 21–2). Such circular churches were normally associated with the Knights Templar and the Knights of St John of Jerusalem, the orders founded to guard the Holy Land and the Holy Sepulchre, though the church in Cambridge has no direct connection with either, but was simply built by the local 'Fraternity of the Holy Sepulchre' of which little is known.

The building of these religious foundations at Cambridge during the twelfth century reflects the prosperity of the town at that time and also shows the beginnings of an academic community: such monastic institutions were the

centres of learning long before universities came about. Further religious foundations were established throughout the thirteenth century, many of which formed the basis of future colleges at the time of the Reformation and the Dissolution of the Monasteries under Henry VIII some three centuries later.

Domesday Book, the great survey of England made under William the Conqueror in 1086, records that most of the dense woodland in the Cambridge area had been cleared, the open field system of communal cultivation was well organised, parish boundaries had been created and law and order firmly enforced by the new Norman overlords. Cambridge was now flourishing as an important commercial centre and it was from this point on that the military importance of the place was no longer paramount, and the lower east bank area began to develop as the main town, rather than the dominating higher ground on the north-west bank.

The boundaries of the medieval town were precisely defined. For defensive purposes the King's Ditch had been dug around the east and south sides, while the loop of the river offered protection to the north and west. The thriving town was contained within these boundaries, and the military settlement on the west bank to the north was now quickly becoming its first suburb. However, the flood plain of the river still constituted a large area in the town which could not be built upon, and in order to overcome this the townsmen took drastic action. The river was diverted on a new course along the eastern edge of its flood plain (the original route was probably further to the west near the present Queen's Road), and this allowed the construction of essential riverside buildings along the now harder east bank nearer the town centre. As a result a new commercial area arose between the river and the High Street (now St John's Street, Trinity Street, King's Parade and Trumpington

20

Street), dissected by a network of lanes and hythes which connected the busy wharves with the town centre and marketplace, the names reflecting the goods unloaded at the quaysides, such as Cornhythe, Salthythe and Flaxhythe. By this time the busy port had now spread far upstream covering the whole area from what is now Magdalene Bridge in the north right along to the Mill Pool in the south. The flood plain of the river had now been successfully confined to the west bank and its rich, alluvial soils were later to form the Backs.

This clever reorganisation of the centre gave new impetus to the now thriving market town, though any further expansion in the future would be limited to east and west owing to the existence of the two great fields on either side; the Barnwell Field to the east, and the Cambridge Field to the west. The open field system of cultivation existed in every English town, forming an essential part of the livelihood of the medieval community, but normally there was only one great field, and it is thought that at Cambridge two fields evolved owing to the dual origins of the town. It is still possible in places to trace the medieval farming system on the west side of the city, but the east side has been heavily developed since Victorian times, though a few areas of common land have survived from the great east field: the long tract of land that penetrates almost into the centre along the south bank of the river as Stourbridge Common, Midsummer Common and Jesus Green (fig. 23).

Academic Invaders

In the early years of the thirteenth century the burgesses of the town had been campaigning for the 'freedom' of the borough from the Crown. This was at last successfully achieved in 1207 only two years before the conjectured

21

21. The Church of the Holy Sepulchre at Cambridge, or the 'Round Church', is one of only five such round churches in the country to survive fairly intact. It was built sometime in the second quarter of the twelfth century, but was considerably altered in the fifteenth century when a polygonal, battlemented bell tower was added. That was replaced with the current stone vault above the clerestory during a major Victorian restoration in 1841–3, at which time the Norman windows were rebuilt based on an example surviving from the original building.

22. Fish-eye view of the circular nave of the Round Church, showing the dominant feature in Romanesque architecture, the semicircular arch, here decorated with characteristic patterning on the arches and capitals.

22

23. *Cambridge from the west. This view shows how compact Cambridge is, with the countryside from the east penetrating right into the city centre via the tract of land flanking the river as Stourbridge Common, Midsummer Common and Jesus Green (visible to the left of the picture). Cambridge airport can be seen in the middle distance. The park in the centre is Christ's Pieces and New Square, to the right of which is Parker's Piece with Fenner's cricket ground beyond to its right. The central range of colleges is in the foreground, with the Backs running along the bottom of the picture. The colleges along the Backs are, from left to right: St John's, Trinity, Trinity Hall (with Gonville & Caius behind), Clare, King's, Queens' (with St Catharine's, Corpus Christi and Pembroke behind). Colleges across the centre of the picture are, from left to right: Jesus College with its extensive on-site playing fields, Sidney Sussex just below the spire of All Saints Church, Christ's in the middle, below the trees on Christ's Pieces, Emmanuel between Christ's Pieces and Parker's Piece, and to the far right, below Parker's Piece, the large open court of Downing. Great St Mary's Church and the market square are in the lower middle of the picture.*

23

date of the founding of the university, an event that was to be comparable in its effect on the town to any of the previous invasions. Although the townspeople thought they had gained their autonomy, they were soon to find that they had a new master in the powerful university authorities to whom they would play the subservient host for many centuries to come.

The very first university was founded in Bologna in 1088. This was followed by one in Paris in 1170, on which Oxford was directly modelled and well established by 1200 with a leading theologian, John Grim, as its main official. Interestingly, Grim was a native of Cambridge and many of his academic friends at Oxford also came from the Cambridge area. The origins of the university at Cambridge are somewhat obscure. There are amusing legends that attribute its found-ing to Cantaber, a mythical Spanish prince born in Athens, who is said to have set up a school here in which Pythagoras taught, or to Sigebert, King of the East Angles, who created it in the Dark Ages. But the earliest authentic date that the place is recorded as a centre of learning is 1209 when, as a result of riots in Oxford, a group of scholars fled from there, headed by John Grim, and established themselves in Cambridge. In 1229 a further group of students left Paris under similar circumstances and also migrated to Cambridge. It was around this time that the university and its Chancellor were legally recognised. No further English universities were founded for over six hundred years and why, in the early thirteenth century, anyone should want to form a university in a little market town on the edge of the desolate East Anglian Fens is difficult to understand. Perhaps this very isolation was its main attraction, making it a safe harbour, along with the fact that the town already pos-sessed a learned community in the form of the religious houses. It would not be unreasonable to assume that the academic migrants from Oxford and Paris came in the knowledge that an intellectual society of teachers already existed there.

The university has not always lived in close harmony with its host the town, and for many centuries there was much friction between the academic community and the townspeople or, as it came to be known, between 'Town' and 'Gown'. The grievances between the two parties seem to have arisen because neither side was really willing to tolerate the other. Originally, owing to the definition of a scholar and to what was then termed the 'Benefit of Clergy' – which could effectively be claimed by anyone who could read and write – many undesirable characters came to the town in the guise of scholars and often gave the genuine academics a bad reputation with the townspeople. Conversely, the well-intentioned scholar often suffered from the extortionate rents charged by local landlords – the present-day situation of students living in their colleges or in college-owned property did not come about until the fifteenth century.

As the university became more established its powers were gradually increased to take in such things as weights and measures and ale-house licensing, which must have been particularly hard for the townsmen to swallow. Apart from such minor, everyday irritations, there were other far more serious occurrences which led to rioting and even the hanging of townsmen, while the often equally guilty academics got off lightly. The university became all powerful within the town, and soon the Chancellor and the Masters of the colleges gained the right to try all civil and criminal cases in which a clerk (teacher) was either plaintiff or defendant. This was officially named the Chancellor's Court, but it soon became known as 'The Townsmen's Scourge', as undoubtedly many academics took advantage of the protection it afforded. Things continued to worsen between Town and Gown, and a particularly bad riot in 1261 resulted in damage to many houses and the burning of university records. When the case was tried by three judges appointed by Henry III, sixteen townsmen and twenty-eight scholars were found guilty. The scholars received the King's pardon, but the townsmen were all hanged for inciting the riot.

Without the university Cambridge would not be the place it is today, in either stature or architecture. However, it was not the university itself that had such an impact on the townscape, but the gradual evolution of the individual colleges, of which there are now more than thirty. Although the functions of the university and its associated colleges are interrelated, the two have developed along quite separate lines architecturally. In fact, until the mid-nineteenth century, when it was forced to expand its teaching and administrative facilities owing to the introduction of many new subjects into the curriculum, the university only had a comparatively minor architectural presence within the town. The first purpose-built university building – the Divinity School (fig. 24) – was begun in the second half of the fourteenth century. This was followed by the Schools of Law and Arts and the Old University Library, all of which

were functioning by about 1475 and today form part of the quadrangle known as the Old Schools (fig. 25). Almost 250 years then passed before any further purpose-built university buildings were erected, when James Gibbs built the Senate House in 1722–30 next door to the Old Schools. A few other buildings were then added here up to the early years of Queen Victoria's reign. So over a period of more than 400 years the only area of university development was in this relatively small precinct, just off the market square to the immediate north of the massive King's College Chapel, which dominated the university court over which it towers. The nineteenth- and early twentieth-century expansion of university buildings in the town made its presence almost as dominant as that of the colleges, and although architecturally the result was vast in quantity it was, on the whole, fairly poor in quality. The main area of development in that period was concentrated to the north and south of Pembroke and Downing Streets, as the New Museums Site and the Downing Site respectively. The majority of post-1945 development took place initially in the southern area of the town, around Trumpington Street and Lensfield Road, and then

24. The oldest university building in Cambridge, the Divinity School (c.1350–1400).

25. The Old Schools precinct from the tower of Great St Mary's Church. The Senate House and its lawn are in the foreground, the classical eighteenth-century front of the Old Schools medieval Cobble Court facing, with the nineteenth-century University Library to its north (now the library of Gonville & Caius College), and beyond is the former King's College Old Court with its gatehouse. King's College Chapel is to the left and, in the far distance, is the tower of the modern University Library, west of the river.

24

25

26. *King's College Chapel from the tower of Great St Mary's Church. This view shows the massive Perpendicular Gothic chapel with the nineteenth-century Gothic Revival gatehouse and screen fronting King's Parade.*

26

27. *St John the Evangelist above the entrance arch of the gatehouse, St John's College, with the heraldic arms of Lady Margaret Beaufort, the founder of the college, below.*

28 *(right). Henry VIII, the founder of the college, on the gatehouse of Trinity. This 'wretched statue' (Pevsner) was carved in 1615 by William Cure the Younger, and the current wooden chair leg held by the king replaces a missing sceptre.*

29. *The Old Library, St John's College (1623–4), by Henry Man.*

30. *Senior dons in King's Parade, dressed in scarlet, having just left official ceremonies at the Senate House.*

31. Nevile's Gate, Trinity College (1597–1605), named after Dr Thomas Nevile, who was elected Master of the College in 1593.

32. King's College Chapel from Queen's Road.

31

later to the west of the river on the Sidgwick Avenue site and to the south of Madingley Road. The contemporary pattern of both university and college expansion has been to abandon the packed city centre and to build in the more spacious areas to the west. There is no single building, or group of buildings, at Cambridge that can be referred to as 'the university', and the buildings that comprise it – its faculties and laboratories, library, administrative and ceremonial buildings – are dispersed throughout the city and around its perimeter. These, along with the colleges, make Cambridge one huge campus.

By the time the original university buildings were completed in the last quarter of the fifteenth century, a dozen colleges had already been established (see summary on pp.188–9) and their presence soon began to dominate the town. The first was founded in 1280 by Hugh de Balsham, Bishop of Ely, when he arranged to house his endowed scholars with the monks at the Hospital of St John. This was unsuccessful and in 1284 the academics moved to their own building just outside the city boundary, south of the Trumpington Gate, next to the Church of St Peter (now St Mary the Less). This establishment subsequently came to be known as Peterhouse. The Bishop based his foundation on Merton, the first official college at Oxford founded by Walter de Merton in 1264. It is interesting to note that Merton also owned property in Cambridge, on what is now the site of St John's College towards Northampton Street, and it may only have been by chance that he chose to found his college on his land in Oxford rather than in Cambridge. The hall (1286) was the first building at Peterhouse (fig. 33), and is the oldest surviving collegiate structure in the city. No further colleges were founded until the fourteenth century when seven were established in less than thirty years. These early colleges were quite different from those of the present day, as they were endowed foundations housing only teachers and there were no students resident in them. It was only following the innovative ideas of William of Wykeham at Oxford in 1379, when he founded his 'New College' there, that provision was made for the unqualified students to live in the colleges under the care of graduates, which is how the term 'undergraduate' came about.

It was not the responsibility of the university to found colleges. These were the result of benefactions from wealthy individuals who, until the nineteenth century, tended to be royalty, the nobility, the clergy or the more wealthy and powerful civil servants. At Cambridge there have been two exceptions to this: in 1352 two town guilds came together to establish the College of Corpus Christi and the Blessed Virgin Mary, the only instance of the people of Cambridge founding a college until 1974 when a local businessman, Mr David Robinson, founded the last of the colleges to date

33. The hall at Peterhouse (c.1286–90), the oldest surviving collegiate building in Cambridge. Along with the rest of Old Court at Peterhouse, the hall was ashlared (stone-faced) by James Burrough in 1754–5 and further restored by George Gilbert Scott in 1870, thus hiding the original brick and rubble construction on the court side.

33

in his name. The reforming spirit of the later nineteenth century saw a change in the way that colleges came about when Girton, Newnham and Hughes Hall resulted directly from the fight for the equality of women and the right to further education. In the same spirit, New Hall and Lucy Cavendish followed in the mid-twentieth century, offering an even broader opportunity for women at Cambridge before co-education finally began to infiltrate the mass of all-male colleges from the early 1960s.

The birth of the early colleges coincided with a decline in the river trade at Cambridge and, subsequently, in the prosperity of the town. This was the case up and down the country as a whole, partly due to the continual drain of national funds in heavy taxation to finance the Hundred Years War with France between 1337 and 1453. Also, the Black Death was very severe in the eastern counties in the middle years of the fourteenth century and Cambridge was not a particularly healthy place to live at this time. Its location on the edge of the marshy Fens, combined with hot summers recorded from this period, made it extremely vulnerable to disease. There was a regular flow of traders and scholars through the town, who probably acted as carriers for the plague, and its sanitary arrangements were greatly neglected. This was a major grievance of the university authorities, who tried on several occasions to force the Corporation to improve the situation and, in particular, to clean out the King's Ditch, which had virtually become an open sewer encompassing the whole east and south sides of the town. For several years the mortality rate at Cambridge was extremely high. The town was deserted by traders, while the academics often vacated the university in the summer months to live in the country away from the Black Death, which took its toll on many of their colleagues. For instance, in the summer of 1349 sixteen of the forty scholars of King's Hall (later part of Trinity College) died of

the plague. In 1402 an order was finally passed in an attempt to combat the pestilence that was now associated with the town, but it fell far short of what the university authorities wanted, only stating that no dung or filth was allowed to be left in the streets or marketplace for more than seven days. This was a harsh time for all, but it gave the colleges the opportunity to establish a strong presence in the area between the wharves and the High Street in the wake of the decline of the river industry. Town and Gown feuds continued throughout this period. The Peasants' Revolt of 1381, which started in Kent and Essex, quickly spread east and north, reaching Cambridge in June, and it gave the townspeople the opportunity to express their grievances against the increasingly dominant university. During the two days of rioting, the angry mob, led by many of the town's officials, forced the university authorities and the Masters of the colleges to renounce their privileges and to abide by the laws common to all. The rioters broke into Great St Mary's Church, which had been taken over by the university as its administrative headquarters, and statutes, charters and other effects of the university and colleges were publicly burnt in the marketplace. The revolt in the Cambridge area was suppressed by Henry le Spencer, Bishop of Norwich, with a small troop of soldiers. In the following November, the Mayor and Bailiffs of the town were summoned to Westminster where their forcibly obtained concessions were declared void and they were severely reprimanded for their actions against the scholars.

A major fire in the town centre in 1385 saw the destruction of more than a hundred houses, leaving many townspeople homeless and adding to the general exodus that had followed the years of plague. The fifteenth century then saw the foundation of six new colleges, and by far the most controversial of these, and undoubtedly the most important single event in the topographical history of medieval

34. *Bread stall in the market.*

35. *Market Square from the tower of Great St Mary's Church. This view to the east looks over Cambridge centre in a direction which excludes any major academic buildings, apart from the rooftops of Christ's College just below the trees. The Petty Cury shopping precinct can be seen to the right, just beyond the far right corner of the market stalls. The spire to the left is that of Holy Trinity Church.*

34

36. *Flower stall, Market Square.*

37

37. *Fruit and vegetable stall, with Great St Mary's Church behind.*

Cambridge, was King's College, in 1441. This royal foundation by Henry VI was eventually to stretch from the High Street in the east to the river in the west, and from Clare College in the north to the then site of the Carmelite Friars in the south, now Queens' College. This was a huge area for a single foundation and it was right in the middle of the town in one of its busiest localities, bustling with life and crowded with tenements and commercial properties dissected by streets connecting the marketplace to the busy wharves of the riverside.

The King's acquisition of this site for his college effectively divorced the commercial town centre from the river in that area, dealing yet another severe blow to the ailing river trade. At this time a major street, Milne Street, ran through this area parallel to the High Street and the river on a line that today would be the continuation of Queens' Lane in

the south to Trinity Lane in the north. The central section of Milne Street, and all the properties around it, were demolished to make way for the college, and to compensate the town for depriving it of its access to the river in this area the King gave some land to the north of his site upon which the corporation created alternative access via what is now Garret Hostel Lane between Trinity Hall and Trinity College.

The foundation of King's College marked the transition of the town centre at Cambridge from civic to academic control. However, Henry was still not satisfied with the potential limitations of his site on the east bank and, perhaps with foresight for his bigger vision and grand design, he later also acquired a large area of the immediately adjacent west bank in 1447. With regard to Cambridge as we know it today this was another very important step as that piece of land, now comprising the water meadows of King's – known

38 and 39. Great St Mary's Church from the market square in the east and King's Parade in the west.

as Scholars' Piece (fig. 186) – inaugurated the eventual creation of the Backs. These are the back gardens of seven of the oldest colleges that either run down to, or traverse, the river. (The modern Darwin College could also be included in this group as its garden backs on to the river around the Mill Pool area.)

Henry VI did not live to see the completion of his college, eventually going insane and being murdered in the Tower of London on the orders of Edward IV in 1471 during the Wars of the Roses. Although possibly the most unfortunate of medieval English kings, with little achievement to his name, he is remembered largely for his dual educational foundations of Eton College near Windsor, and King's College at Cambridge. Once again, developments at Oxford played an important role here and Henry modelled his foundations on the ideas of William of Wykeham. Having completed the building of his New College in six years without interruption in 1380–6, Wykeham, who was Bishop of Winchester, went on to build Winchester College, in Hampshire, in 1387–93 as the school from which the scholars would then proceed to their university education at his Oxford college. Similarly, Henry established Eton College in 1440, and then King's a year later, with the same intention of his scholars progressing from Eton to Cambridge. Cardinal Wolsey did the same again at Oxford in 1525 when he established Cardinal College, linking it with his grammar school at Ipswich.

The building of King's College itself was very spasmodic and it was many years after Henry's death before the chapel was completed, with the site as we know it today not being finished until the twentieth century. The establishment of the college on such a large site in the middle of the town, coupled with the plague epidemics and the great fire of 1385, resulted in a marked decline in the population. The townsfolk were very disaffected and in 1446 the burgesses complained that houses previously occupied by artisans were now taken by scholars and, as a consequence of the vastly increased influx of academics, many local people were now leaving the district.

The transition from market town to academic centre was now having a particularly noticeable effect on the town's architecture. The fifteenth century saw the construction of some of the finest Cambridge buildings: King's College Chapel, the original first courts at Queens', Magdalene and Pembroke Colleges, and much at Gonville Hall and Trinity Hall. Also, an extensive rebuilding scheme was undertaken at this time on Great St Mary's (1478–1608), which was by then known as the University Church (fig. 39). In stark contrast, building activity in the town itself was almost at a standstill, and although many of the local parish churches were being enlarged, those additions were simply to house the increased congregations brought about by the large numbers of new scholars living in the steadily evolving colleges. It was the increase in these foundations, from this point on, that had such an impact on the townscape and, as they grew, in both size and number, they began to dominate the town centre. (For a more detailed analysis of the development of the college plan, see page 139.)

Reformation Cambridge

After the dramatic exploits of one King Henry at Cambridge, those of another soon followed: Henry VIII, who acceded to the throne in 1509. By 1534 the divorce of the Church of England from Rome was complete, and after the Dissolution of the Monasteries an Act was passed in 1545 authorising the similar suppression of the colleges of both Oxford and Cambridge as they were seen as religious foundations. The university authorities in Cambridge acted

40. *King's College Chapel from the north, dominating the centre of Cambridge, with the fields of south Cambridgeshire beyond.*

40

41. *King's College Chapel, east end of the nave.*

42. *King's College Chapel, west elevation.*

One of the most important examples of English medieval architecture, and the most famous building in Cambridge, King's College Chapel was begun in 1446 by the founder of the college, Henry VI, and continued through the reigns of the five following monarchs to reach final completion under Henry VIII in 1515.

This stunning building was not modelled on previous college chapels, but on the bigger scale of the cathedral choir, and the resulting interior is breathtaking. The nave is a single vaulted space of twelve bays, the beautifully elegant fan vault being the largest of its kind in existence. This massive Perpendicular structure (the vault is estimated to weigh 1,875 tons) creates an impression of almost unbelievable weightlessness, with its many curved stone ribs seeming to float unaided nearly a hundred feet above the ground.

The huge stained glass windows of the nave, mainly the work of Flemish glaziers in 1517–31, depict Biblical scenes. The powerful masterpiece The Adoration of the Magi, *by Peter Paul Rubens, is situated at the east end, given to the college in 1961.*

The dramatic space of the nave of King's College Chapel, divided by the organ and screen.

43. View across the choir stalls from the east end.

44 and **45.** Details of the wooden angels with trumpets on top of the organ.

46. View from the west showing the screen at its most powerful.

43

44

45

46

quickly and sought the help of Catherine Parr, Henry's sixth wife, a campaign that evidently succeeded. The King was lenient, and not only excused the colleges, but also established his own foundation at Cambridge, Trinity College. However, the religious houses in the town, such as Barnwell Priory, the oldest and richest of the local monastic institutions, did have to yield, and many of them were later incorporated into existing or new college foundations. These included the two Elizabethan colleges of Emmanuel (formerly the site of the Dominican Priory) and Sidney Sussex (the Franciscan Priory). Henry founded Trinity in 1546 to be, of course, the largest of the colleges at Cambridge and, it is thought, to outdo his then Lord Chancellor, Thomas Wolsey, who had founded his own Cardinal College at Oxford in 1525. Cardinal College was eventually to be taken over by Henry and transformed into Christ Church at about the same time as the founding of Trinity. In order to establish his Cambridge foundation, the King combined the existing colleges of Michaelhouse (founded by Hervey de Stanton in 1324) and King's Hall (founded by Edward III in 1337), along with other properties in the vicinity.

By the early sixteenth century Cambridge had sunk to the twenty-ninth wealthiest town in England, as calculated by its tax contributions. However, by the middle of the next century it had risen to ninth wealthiest. This was a result of the temporary recovery of the English river trade, which culminated in the golden age of river transport in the eighteenth century before its final collapse in the nineteenth owing to the coming of the railways. This newfound prosperity was largely based on agricultural productivity in this rich corner of the country, and Cambridge was one of London's major corn markets during the reign of Elizabeth I (1558–1603). The Reformation had also seen the development of a few industries introduced into the town by the university, such as book production and its associated

crafts. Bookselling was a major trade in the city in general and, in particular, at the famous Stourbridge Fair held every summer in the area of what is now Midsummer and Stourbridge Commons to which traders came from all over Europe buying and selling an array of goods. Many bookbinders operated in Cambridge in the early sixteenth century, such as one called Garret Godfrey, a friend of Erasmus, the Dutch humanist, who was teaching in the university at the time. The first Cambridge printer, Johann van Lair of Siegberg, near Cologne, was also operating in the early 1520s after settling in the city. Hops had been introduced into eastern England from the Netherlands at the end of the previous century, and by the early 1550s Cambridge had its first major brewery, located by the river near Magdalene College and run by a Dutchman named Francis van Hoorn. There is an excellent illustration of Cambridge by John Hammond of 1592 showing what the centre of the town was like at this time (fig. 47).

Seventeenth- and Eighteenth-Century Cambridge

Cambridge was actively involved in the Civil War (1642–51), which gave added venom to the age-old feud between Town and Gown – the townspeople were Parliamentarian, the academics predominantly Royalist. It was widely known that the colleges were often used to store munitions for the Royalists, and scholars walked the streets in fear of attack by the locals, unable to leave the town unless they could produce a voucher signed by a leading townsman stating that they were a 'confider' and sympathetic to the Parliamentarian cause.

Oliver Cromwell, himself a native of the eastern counties, had been elected Member of Parliament for Cambridge in 1640 and was no stranger to the place, as he had been an undergraduate at Sidney Sussex College. Once again, Cambridge became an important strategic and military stronghold, this time controlling the roads between East Anglia and the Midlands, rather than simply the river crossing, though a large cannon called a 'drake' was placed on Magdalene Bridge in defence of the town. Several of the other bridges were destroyed by Cromwell's men to hinder

a possible attack by Royalist forces. Such an attack was thought to be imminent in February 1643 when Cromwell raised an army of 30,000 men to protect Cambridge, but this turned out to be a false alarm and, in fact, no such attack ever took place.

The most important topographical event of this period was when the large and rather muddled site of Trinity

47. *John Hammond's aerial perspective of Cambridge drawn in 1592. Note, in particular, that the sites of King's, Trinity and St John's are all in their old states, as are the smaller colleges of Clare Hall, Trinity Hall and Caius. The area to the west of Bridge Street can also be seen in its original state, prior to early twentieth-century development.*

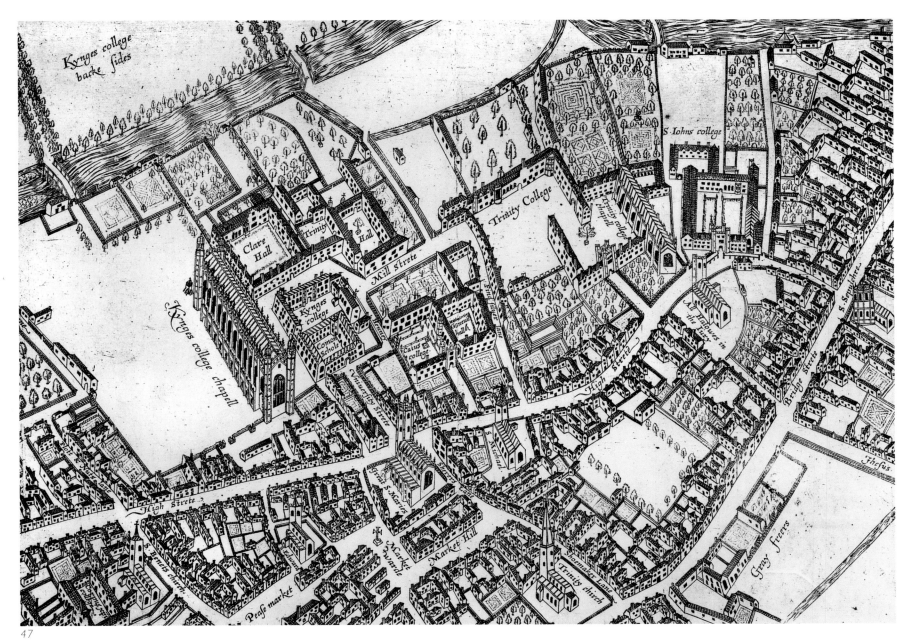

47

48. The Backs in winter, with Clare College Bridge in the foreground and King's College Bridge beyond. Clare Bridge is the oldest bridge over the river (1638–40) and was one of the earliest examples of classical architecture to appear at Cambridge, built, and probably designed, by the local mason, Thomas Grumbold.

48

49

49. Trinity College Bridge was built in 1764–5 by the local architect James Essex, its predecessor of 1651–2 having been demolished and used to create the new substructure below water level. It is faced in Portland and Ketton stone ashlar. The avenue of lime trees beyond creates a grand approach to the rear of the college from Queen's Road (fig. 83), once over the bridge entering past Christopher Wren's magnificent college library (fig. 64).

50. Queens' College Bridge or, as it is commonly known, the Mathematical Bridge, was designed in 1749 by an undergraduate, W. Etheridge, and constructed by James Essex in 1749–50. Etheridge travelled widely and was clearly inspired here by a visit to China while a student at the college. The bridge has been rebuilt twice, in 1867 and 1902, and the story goes that the original was completely void of any metal fixings, being entirely self-supporting.

College was reorganised and transformed between 1597 and 1605 by its Master, Dr Thomas Nevile. This was a huge task, which Nevile executed with great planning ingenuity, resulting in one of the town's most famous compositions, Great Court (fig. 51). A few years later, in 1610 and 1613 respectively, St John's College and Trinity College purchased land from the town on both sides of the river as a continuation of their existing sites to the west, Trinity giving to the town the area that is now Parker's Piece in exchange. At this time Clare College also purchased from King's the northern section of its water meadows site on the west bank, enabling it to extend its site west across the river too. These acquisitions extended the college Backs. In 1615, Dr Stephen Perse, a Fellow of Gonville & Caius College, died, but not before founding a 'Free School' in what is now Free School Lane, and this was later to become the Perse Grammar School, the forerunner of the current independent school now on Hills Road. When Dr John Addenbrooke, another famous Cambridge man, died in 1719, he left £4,500 in his will for the founding of a hospital, and the first

Addenbrooke's was built on Trumpington Street in 1740 (now the Judge Institute of Management Studies). The last outbreaks of the plague occurred in the middle years of the seventeenth century, after which the town was not troubled again by serious pestilence. However, it still was not until 1788 that an Act was finally passed to ensure the regular cleansing of the town's sanitary system, and at this time lamps were also installed along Cambridge streets. There are three excellent volumes of illustrations showing seventeenth- and eighteenth-century Cambridge: Loggan's *Cantabrigia Illustrata* (1690), Harraden's *Cantabrigia Depicta* (1811), and Ackerman's *History of Cambridge University* (1815).

During this time there was very little enlargement of the medieval town, even though the population almost doubled. This confinement was largely due to the great fields to east and west, and the increase in population was simply accommodated by increasing the density of the built-up area. Some contemporary eyewitness reports are revealing: 'The buildings in many parts of the town were so little and so low that they looked more like huts for pigmies than houses for

51. Great Court at Trinity College, the largest Oxbridge composition measuring 257 feet (N) x 288 feet (S) x 325 feet (E) x 340 feet (W). This view shows the northern half of the court, with the following buildings making up the ranges (from west to east, left to right): the tall bay window of Nevile's Hall, the Master's Lodge, the Old Library building as the west end of the north range (one of the earliest three-storey buildings in Cambridge, 1554–5), King Edward's Tower, the chapel and the gatehouse. The free-standing fountain is in the foreground, and the chapel of St John's College, next door, can be seen in the distance.

51

men. The place is not at all large and about as mean as a village, and were it not for the many fine colleges it would be one of the sorriest places in the world.' No new colleges were founded throughout this period, though there was much building activity and expansion. Until then the colleges had kept a fairly discreet profile, their enclosed courtyards being on a domestic scale, the only exception being the accepted audacity of Henry VI with his huge, though superb, chapel at King's which dominated the town as it still does today. The only emphasis given to the street façades of the colleges were the towered gatehouses that appeared from the fifteenth century onwards, and by 1600 there were nine of these sturdy structures scattered throughout the town (figs 52–60). From the Tudor period, classical details

and complete classical structures (such as the organ screen in King's College Chapel – figs 43, 46), though not yet entire buildings, started to appear in Cambridge and college buildings were gradually to become more elegant and ornate over the next two centuries. Those responsible for commissioning the new buildings, the Masters and Fellows of the colleges, began to change their requirements from simple, utilitarian domestic buildings to house academics, to those creating a fashionable public display, particularly in their street façades.

It was not until 1640–3 that the first predominantly classical building was erected, the Fellows' Building at Christ's College (fig. 61). The architect of this building is unknown, and although it was unique in Cambridge at the time, and

52–60. *College gatehouses existing by the year 1600.*
52. *King Edward's Tower at Trinity (1427–37), the prototype Cambridge gatehouse.*
53. *The gatehouse of the former King's College Old Court (now the university Old Schools precinct), begun in 1441, but only half built and not completed until the nineteenth century.*
54. *Queens' College gatehouse (1448). The actual entrance through the gatehouse has an original lierne vault made from local clunch limestone.*
55. *Jesus College gatehouse (c. 1500), unlike its counterparts, a less fortified structure lacking the strong corner accentuations of the building type.*
56 and 57. *Christ's and St John's gatehouses, (1505 and 1511). Both of these colleges were founded by Lady Margaret Beaufort and bear her very decorative coat of arms.*
58. *The Great Gate at Trinity (1518–35), unique amongst the Cambridge gatehouses as it contains a main entrance arch flanked by a smaller pedestrian doorway.*
59. *The Queen's Gate at Trinity (1596–7), with a statue of Queen Elizabeth I at its centre.*
60. *The Shrewsbury Tower at St John's (1598–1602), named after the Countess of Shrewsbury whose statue stands in the recess above the arch.*

52

53

54

55

56

57

58

59

60

61

61. Fellows' Building, Christ's College, stylistically the most important building of the mid-seventeenth century at Cambridge as it introduced the Renaissance idea of a balanced composition, long, low and symmetrical. The detailing of this building was almost entirely classical, though reference to the past could still be seen in the four-centred arch of the central gateway. The classical dormers in the roof were particularly innovative.

62–64. The three buildings of Christopher Wren at Cambridge. 62. Pembroke College Chapel, Wren's first completed building. 63. Emmanuel College Chapel. Here, the composition is rather more baroque with the entablature projecting at the centre, and the pediment broken and penetrated by the base of the cupola which contains the clock. 64. Wren's main Cambridge building, Trinity College Library, which had a great influence on the local designers and set the standard for much of the collegiate and university architecture that was to follow.

innovative in the country as a whole, it still referred in certain details to medieval forms. In the 1660s Cambridge received its first wholly classical building with Christopher Wren's Pembroke College Chapel of 1663–5 (fig. 62). This was Wren's first completed work of architecture (the Sheldonian Theatre at Oxford had been begun slightly earlier in 1663, but was not finished until 1669). This was followed by his chapel at Emmanuel in 1668–74 (figs 63, 69) and then by Wren's Cambridge masterpiece in 1676–95, Trinity College Library (fig. 64). The influence of Wren on the local architects and designers was immense and can be seen in many other buildings of this period.

The early eighteenth century was a time of great proposals for magnificent building schemes at Cambridge, the likes of

63

64

62

which had not been seen since Henry VI at King's. However, none of these came to be realised in their entirety, and only a few buildings as parts of larger proposals were ever built. The architect James Gibbs suffered from this frustration in two instances at Cambridge, with the Senate House (fig. 65) for the university, and his Fellows, or Gibbs' Building at King's (fig. 68), both only component parts of much grander submissions. Apart from the famous, London-based architects of the day, there were also a few local designers who were now competent in the new classical manner: Sir James Burrough (an amateur architect and Master of Gonville & Caius College) and James Essex, both of whom added several fine college buildings at this time – Burrough's Building at Peterhouse (fig. 66) and the front of Emmanuel College by Essex (fig. 67). These two architects were also largely responsible for the fashionable trend at this time of

65. The Senate House by James Gibbs of 1722–30, 'a most elegant blend of the English Wren tradition with the new Palladianism' (Pevsner).
66. Burrough's Building at Peterhouse (1738–42), also in a classic Palladian style (i.e. after Andrea Palladio, 1508–80).
67. The front portico of Emmanuel College (1769–75) by James Essex.
68. Gibbs' Building at King's College (1724–32).

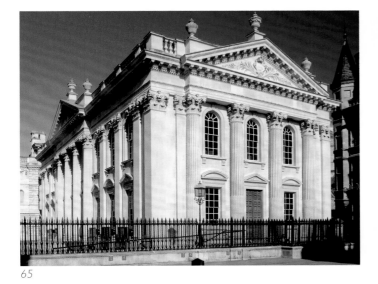

65

66

67

68

69

69. *Emmanuel College Chapel (1668–74) by Sir Christopher Wren.*

70. *A painted dragon decorating the eastern archway of the screens passage, Christ's College.*

71. *Quincentenary procession, Christ's College, 1 May 2005, marking the foundation of the college on 1 May 1505. The picture shows First Court, taken with a fish-eye lens from the upper storey of the gatehouse, with members of the college circumnavigating the court after a service in the chapel to commemorate the founding of the college by Lady Margaret Beaufort, mother of Henry VII. The procession is headed by the college choir and a bishop, followed by the Fellowship, members of the student body and college staff.*

72. *The Master's Lodge, Christ's College. Photographed on 1 May, 2005 on the occasion of the quincentenary celebration to mark the founding of the college (fig. 71).*

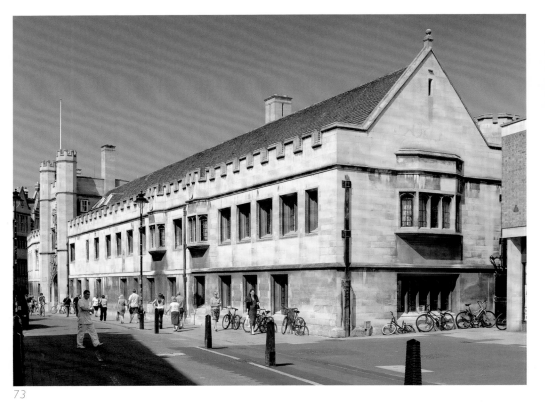

73

74

73. The long façade of Christ's College in St Andrew's Street, originally a Gothic brick building of 1505–11, but refaced in stone in 1758–69.

74. The front of Pembroke College in Trumpington Street, built in brick in 1351–98, but refaced in stone in 1712 (fig. 150).

'ashlaring', the process by which many fine medieval brick buildings in Cambridge were 'Italianised' by dressing them in a façade of stone, as was the case, for instance, at both Christ's (fig. 73) and Pembroke (fig. 74).

Undoubtedly the most fascinating of the proposed eighteenth-century building schemes at Cambridge – and the biggest missed opportunity in the architectural and planning history of the city – was that put forward by Nicholas Hawksmoor, Wren's former assistant and collaborator. In an amazing scheme (fig. 75) Hawksmoor had planned to reorganise the entire town centre along the lines of a classical baroque forum in order to convert what he saw as a congested little market town into something more fitting to what had now become one of the leading universities in Europe. This was a fascinating idea, though it would have involved extensive reconstruction throughout the town centre, but what a different place Cambridge would have been, with a classical grandeur similar to that of Oxford.

The most notable aspect of Hawksmoor's proposal was to open up the old narrow medieval streets of the town, concentrating on the main south-east to north-west axis from Regent Street to Magdalene Bridge (in fact, the old Roman Road through the city, the Via Devana), and on the High Street, from the south end of King's Parade through to the Round Church beyond St John's College. There was to be an enormous gateway at the south-east approach to the city from London, approximately opposite what is now the entrance to Downing College in Regent Street. This was the grand entrance to the town and would have acted, in the true baroque manner, as a prelude to the main theme, the town centre. At the opposite end of this axis there were to be two piazzas, one on each side of Magdalene Bridge, marking the point of exit. As one progressed along this main route, from the triumphal gateway to the piazzas, dramatic vistas would have opened up: firstly by the new emphasis given to what is now the street called Petty Cury, which was to be widened and set in a direct east-west line from Christ's College gatehouse through to the east end of King's College Chapel; secondly, by a new street cut through from the gateway of Sidney Sussex College to the gatehouse of Trinity; and finally, by a much widened St John's Street, which would now visually connect the Round Church with the gatehouse of St John's College. Thus, as one travelled through Cambridge one's attention would be constantly arrested by hints of the magnificent buildings that existed

further into the architectural heart of the town, around which the main theme of the composition was set.

Sadly, this incredible scheme remained on paper and there are no Hawksmoor buildings in Cambridge. However, *The Town of Cambridge As it Ought to be Reformed*, by the late David Roberts and Gordon Cullen, explains Hawksmoor's scheme in detail and, fascinatingly, translates it into visual form (figs 76–81).

75. *Nicholas Hawksmoor's scheme for the re-planning of the centre of Cambridge (c.1714). Hawksmoor intended to open up the narrow streets of the medieval town, creating new spaces and dramatic vistas. The giant entry gate can be seen in the south-east area of the plan, located roughly opposite what are now the gates of Downing College in Regent Street, and the piazzas marking the point of exit are in the north-west on what is now Magdalene Bridge.*

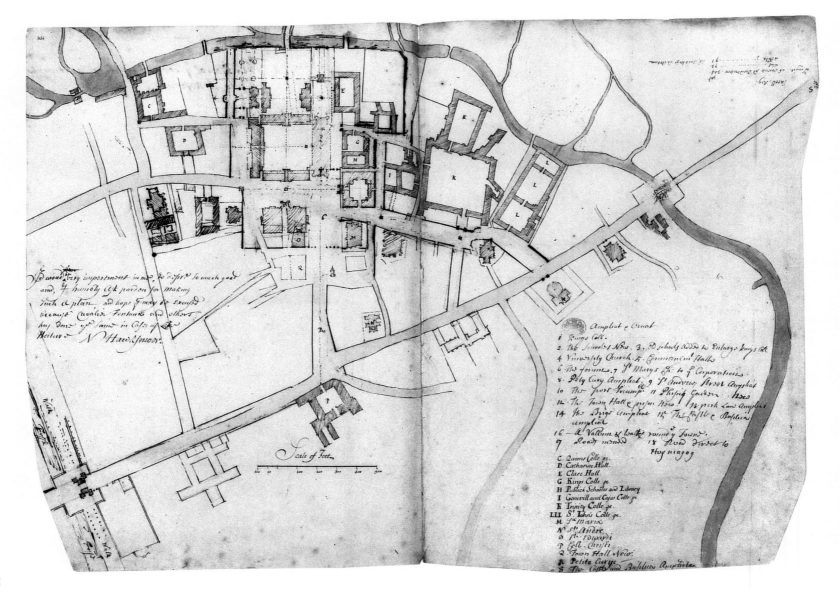

75

76–81. *Modern drawings illustrating Nicholas Hawksmoor's ideas for the centre of Cambridge and what actually exists today.*

76. *The intended university forum, now King's Parade, where the street would have been transformed into a piazza surrounded by grand baroque buildings and,* **77**, *the same area today where the famous Perpendicular Gothic chapel and the nineteenth-century screen face shops and houses opposite.*

78. *The university forum as it would have appeared from the market square, with classical buildings creating dramatic spaces ideal for ceremonial occasions and,* **79**, *the same view today.*

80. *Hawksmoor's idea for the approach towards Trinity College from the forum – another wide and open piazza surrounded by college fronts and shops, wonderfully conceived spaces that would have elevated Cambridge into a beautifully elegant classical city and,* **81**, *the same view down Trinity Street as it is now, tightly enclosed and congested, with Gonville & Caius College to the left, and shops to the right.*

The drawings shown in figs 76, 78 and 80 are reproduced with the permission of the artist, Gordon Cullen.

76

77

78

79

80

81

The Nineteenth Century – Enclosure, Expansion and Reform

The nineteenth century at Cambridge was a time of great change, both in the social and political structure of the town and the university, and in the expansion that was to take place with an acceleration of unprecedented growth. It also saw the beginning of an improved relationship between Town and Gown, when the age of university privileges and its ancient suzerainty over the indigenous population were to be superseded by Act of Parliament. The university itself underwent much internal reform, and the whole academic scene was drastically changed with the introduction of many new subjects into the curriculum, particularly the natural and social sciences in the middle of the century. John Steegman paints a fascinating picture of what student life was probably like at the beginning of this period:

> Byron was up at Trinity [1805–7], boxing, pistol shooting, swimming in the pool above Grantchester which still bears his name, doing little work in the academic sense, but forming close intellectual friendships as well as friendships rather less intellectual but a good deal more passionate… However, this Cambridge of the 'Bucks' of great drinking, of riotous driving of tandems through the narrow streets, of fashionable prize fighters, of privileged noblemen undergraduates, of mail coaches and flying-coaches and stage-coaches, was soon abolished by progress and reform.

The event that was greatly to increase the built-up area of Cambridge at this time was the passing of the Acts of Enclosure, which effectively removed the containing corsets in the form of the great east and west fields in 1802 and 1807 respectively, and resulted in long overdue urban development on all sides. As a result of these Acts of Parliament, the ancient open field system of cultivation was broken down into much smaller units, each being 'enclosed' with hedges, walls or fences, thus creating the patchwork of fields so characteristic of the English countryside today.

By dividing these large areas it was now possible to allocate sections for urban development, and the town started to expand, firstly along the eastern side. Much housing was built between the Newmarket Road to the east and Hills Road to the south, through which a new route, Mill Road, was created. The most intensive period of building took place between the 1820s and 1850s in the area between Hills Road and Trumpington Road, soon to be known as 'New Town'. This new, outer residential district of south and east Cambridge quickly developed its own character, quite different to the old town, the houses consisting mainly of continuous terraces (fig. 82). It thus became a very homogenous area in contrast to the older and much more varied town centre, and it was soon to be joined by similar developments to both the north and south-west.

The population explosion in Cambridge in the nineteenth century was not as great as elsewhere in the country, possibly owing to the lack of local industry, but improved agricultural

82. Typical nineteenth-century terraced housing in the southern area of Cambridge.

82

83. *The Avenue, Trinity College.*

84. *Evening recital, the Old Combination Room, Trinity College.*

83

85. *After the Ball, Trinity College.*

86. *At the Ball, Magdalene College.*

85

GARDE TA FOY

86

production in this extremely fertile corner of England, much of which passed through the Cambridge markets, led, once again, to a renewed prosperity. The Eastern Counties Railway Station was opened in Cambridge in 1845, after much debate about its location. The university authorities eventually won the argument that it should be situated just outside the town to the south-east. This was a deliberate move to make it hard for undergraduates to use the railway and reach the joys of London in a fraction of the time it had taken previously. The location of the station here soon encouraged housing development, even further to the south and east.

The university and its colleges were now the largest single employer in the town, and by the end of the century there were more than twenty colleges housing several thousand Fellows and students, all of whom had to be looked after and fed. Many amenities were supplied to the town at this time, such as gas lighting in the 1820s, a public water supply in 1853, and the first proper drainage system in 1895, before which the river had carried the town's sewage and been a constant health hazard.

The Reform Act of 1832, along with the Municipal Corporations Act of 1835, gave the long-frustrated locals a much greater say in the running of the town. The restructuring of the town's Corporation eventually led to the all-important Cambridge Award Act of 1856. The previous year, a judge in the court of the King's Bench, Sir John Patterson, had been appointed to act as arbitrator to resolve the age-old grievances between Town and Gown. At this time the university was caught up in its own internal problems, trying to bring itself into line with modern subjects and contemporary teaching, and quarrels with its old enemy, the town, must have seemed rather insignificant by comparison. The ancient oaths and declarations binding the Town Council to conserve the privileges and liberties of the university were abolished.

The right of university members to the Chancellor's Court was to cease. The power of the Vice-Chancellor to grant ale-house licences, to supervise weights and measures and the running of markets and fairs, was transferred to the justices of the peace of the borough. Finally, all property of the university and colleges, with a few exceptions, was to be assessed for rates as every other property in the town. A few privileges did remain, but most of these ceased before too long, such as the power of the university authorities to arrest 'common women' whom it considered might be meddling with its undergraduates.

Within the university itself, the fight for equally important reform was also taking place amongst its members, who were trying to shake off many of the now outdated and medieval customs that controlled their lives. Most college statutes required a set number of Fellows to be in religious orders and all Fellows were subject to the Religious Test Act, which excluded dissenters. It is easy to see how such rules were to become a serious problem in the Cambridge of Charles Darwin, whose *Origin of Species* was published in 1859 and encouraged a very controversial form of atheism, particularly amongst the recent influx of natural scientists at that time. Although the anti-subscription movement had been fighting for the repeal of the Test Act since the middle of the eighteenth century, it did not succeed until 1871. Similarly, there was a requirement of celibacy for most of the college Fellows unless, that is, they were the Master of a College, a Professor or a Fellow also holding a university post. Any ordinary Fellow who wished to marry did so at the forfeiture of his Fellowship, as the view of the college was that marriage would only detract from loyalty to the foundation. This issue became a major problem from the mid-nineteenth century until statutes were finally changed in 1882 allowing marriage.

This new breed of Fellows and their families, however, could not be housed within the colleges, and a new type of housing need therefore arose. At the time of Enclosure the university and many of the colleges acquired most of the land west of the river, realising the potential and convenience of this area for later expansion. Unlike other areas around the town, to north, east and south, which were being crammed full of rows of terraced houses, the character of west Cambridge was to be noticeably different and one of comparative wealth (fig. 87). Colleges such as Trinity, St John's, King's and Clare established Fellows' gardens just across the river on the immediate west bank, and then a little further beyond, west of Queen's Road, began to build large detached houses with extensive gardens for dons with private means or rich professionals who could afford to build to the high standards imposed by the colleges through restrictive covenants placed on the building leases. The development of the area was actually initiated by Gonville &

Caius College, the first to grant such building leases on their land in the West Road area. Throughout the Victorian period and into the early twentieth century, many large houses of architectural note were built from Barton Road in the south to Huntingdon Road in the north by such eminent architects as J.J. Stevenson, Basil Champneys, E.S. Prior, Ernest Newton, Baillie Scott, Amian Champneys and Marshall Sisson.

The year 1800 saw the foundation of Downing College, the first new college in Cambridge for more than two hundred years. Downing should have come about in the latter half of the eighteenth century, after the third Sir George Downing died heirless leaving his fortune for the building of the college, but owing to expensive and lengthy litigation by his widow its building was delayed and its scale much diminished. An early Act of Enclosure of 1801, preceding the two main acts of a few years later, provided the site for Downing on the

87. Large, detached housing in the Grange Road area of leafy west Cambridge. These two neo-Georgian/Queen Anne houses were built in 1907 by Amian Champneys, son of Basil Champneys.

87

88. *Cambridge city centre looking south. The buildings in this picture are as follows: part of Trinity College Great Court is in the foreground, with the top of the gatehouse most visible; beyond to the left are Tree Court of Gonville & Caius College, with the tower of Great St Mary's Church immediately behind. To the right, in the middle of the picture, is the back of the Senate House, with King's Parade in front of it, and to the right of the Senate House are the buildings of the university's Old Schools complex, with C.R. Cockerell's Old University Library to the far right (now the library of Gonville & Caius). The towers in the distance are, unmistakably, the eastern half of King's College Chapel to the right, the Pitt Building of Cambridge University Press in the middle distance, with Emmanuel Congregational Church in Trumpington Street to its left. The tower of St Bene't's Church – the oldest building in Cambridge – can just be seen to the right of Great St Mary's, obscured by the tower of Gonville & Caius Tree Court in front of it.*

89. King's College choristers on the way to the chapel from the Choir School for evensong. When the devout Henry VI founded King's College in 1441, he visualised the daily singing of services in the magnificent chapel that he planned to build, and so a choir was established. This event remains an important part in the daily lives of the sixteen choristers who are educated at the college school, a short distance away on the west side of the river.
The world-famous choir also has fourteen choral scholars and two organ scholars, all of whom study a variety of subjects as undergraduates at the college itself.

90. St John's College choristers, New Court Cloister. St John's College has possessed a choir since the seventeenth century, whose main role is the singing of daily services in the college chapel during the university term. The choir is made up of sixteen choristers and four probationers, with the alto, tenor and bass parts being sung by choral scholars who are undergraduates at the college. The choristers are all educated at the college school to the west of the river on Grange Road, which consists of about 450 boys and girls up to the age of 13.

*91. The hall and west range of
Downing College. In the early
nineteenth century William
Wilkins' design for Downing in
a neo-Greek style introduced a
pure clasical revival to Cambridge.
The hall, with its hexastyle
portico, was one of the first
buildings to be built (1818–20).
The chambers adjoining to the
north were originally separate
from the hall, with the connection
being made later which changed
the planning concept of the
designer (see p. 155).*

southern edge of the town centre, an area of marshland previously known as Pembroke Leys, popular for snipe and duck shooting.

Several designs for Downing had been put forward by eminent architects of the day, starting with James Wyatt in 1784. Interestingly, George III had specifically requested that it was not to be a Gothic building. It was eventually designed by a local architect, William Wilkins, and built between 1807 and 1820 in a pure neo-Greek style (fig. 91) as the first

example in Cambridge of the Greek Revival, following on from the Palladian classicism of the previous century. Wilkins was the most prolific collegiate architect of this period in Cambridge, though Downing was his only classical commission in the town (he also designed University College, London, in 1827–8, and the National Gallery in 1834–8).

After Downing, the versatile Wilkins swapped over to the neo-Gothic style for the rest of his Cambridge work, such as New Court at Corpus Christi (1823–7, fig. 92) and

91

the gatehouse and screen at King's (1824–8, fig. 93). The Gothic Revival had already been introduced to Cambridge a couple of years earlier when the architect Sir Jeffry Wyatville redesigned Sidney Sussex College between 1821 and 1833, curiously transforming the original buildings into a neo-Gothic pastiche at the request of the Fellowship, although he had offered to restore sympathetically the genuine Elizabethan Gothic college. The largest and most picturesque neo-Gothic building at Cambridge was New

Court at St John's, by Rickman & Hutchinson of 1826–31 (fig. 94). This Tudor-Gothic composition was the largest single building to that date in Cambridge and the first building by any college on the west bank of the river, connected to the older courts of St John's by the famous Bridge of Sighs, also designed by Henry Hutchinson in 1831. Although in essence a Gothic Revival building, the planning of the composition is classically inspired with its long, symmetrical façade, a mixture not uncommon in other

*92 and **93**. Neo-Gothic work by William Wilkins at Cambridge.*

92. *New Court at Corpus Christi College, one of the most perfect nineteenth-century compositions in the city, with the chapel as its centrepiece.*
93. *The gatehouse and screen at King's College, viewed from the tower of Great St Mary's Church. The prolific Wilkins also designed the east half of the south range at King's, as seen here forming the south side of Front Court, with the hall at its centre containing a most ornate interior (fig. 140).*

94. *New Court, St John's College, by Rickman and Hutchinson, the largest and most picturesque Gothic Revival building at Cambridge, also known as the 'wedding cake'. This wonderful Tudor-Gothic, though classically inspired, composition provides a dramatic backdrop to the northern end of the Backs and it contains a long, and very atmospheric cloistered walk along its entire length to the south (fig. 90).*

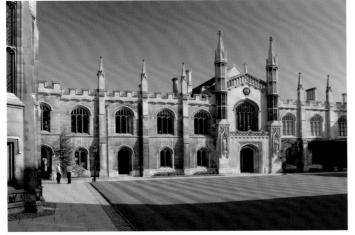

92

93

94

95. *St John's College from the south-west. The Gothic Revival New Court dominates the foreground, with the decorative red-brick gables of Third Court and the Victorian chapel tower beyond. The Bridge of Sighs, which connects the three main college courts to New Court across the river, is hidden behind the large yew tree.*

95

96

96 and **97.** *The Bridge of Sighs, St John's College (1831) by Henry Hutchinson. The bridge takes its name from the bridge in Venice (as does the bridge at Hertford College, Oxford), though there is little similarity in style or design.*

97

98. *Henry VIII at King's College, located in the nineteenth-century street façade, looking down on King's Parade.*

99. *The gatehouse, King's College. This Gothic Revival gatehouse was built in 1824–8 by William Wilkins as part of the screen to King's Parade.*

mid-nineteenth century buildings, such as the Houses of Parliament. A few decades later St John's also built another mammoth Gothic Revival building with their chapel of 1863–9 by the great Victorian Gothicist Sir George Gilbert Scott (fig. 166). However, the purest example of the Gothic Revival at Cambridge from English sources was All Saints Church in Jesus Lane of 1863–71 by G.F. Bodley (fig. 100).

The beginning of the Victorian age at Cambridge also saw a marked stylistic jump within the classical spectrum away from the purity of the Greek Revival at Downing, to the comparative flamboyance of the baroque with two university buildings begun right at the start of Victoria's

100. *The Gothic Revival All Saints Church, Jesus Lane (1863–71), by G. F. Bodley. The original church of All Saints in the Jewry was located in St John's Street, opposite St John's College, and dated back to the eleventh century. It was demolished in 1865 when the street was widened. G.F. Bodley had been the first pupil of the eminent Victorian Gothicist, George Gilbert Scott, under whom he had received a thorough training between 1845 and 1850, essentially as a church architect. Bodley's first design for the new church drew heavily on French sources (as did Scott, interestingly, with his new chapel for St John's College at the same time) and was rejected. However, this second design was hailed as a great success as it concentrated on English models, in particular fourteenth-century parish churches as reflected in its dramatically tall spire. There is much decorative stencilling work in the church by Morris & Co., and the stained glass – notably the east window – includes work by Morris, Burne-Jones and Ford Madox Brown. The church is now redundant.*

100

reign in 1837: the former University Library by C.R. Cockerell (now the library of Gonville & Caius College), and the Fitzwilliam Museum by George Basevi (fig. 101). The Fitzwilliam, in particular, is a prime example of Victorian baroque, designed by one of the leading architects of the day. Basevi, however, did not live to see its completion as he tragically fell to his death in 1845 while inspecting the western tower of Ely Cathedral. Cockerell then took over the work at the Fitzwilliam, which was eventually completed by E.M. Barry in 1875.

Downing was the last of the old, traditional colleges. The next group of foundations that arose in the second half of the nineteenth century was born from a definite need, rather than from beneficence. At Cambridge, the fight for women's emancipation was associated with the cause of higher education for all. Three women's colleges arose: Newnham and Girton – both located away from the male colleges in the town centre for reasons of Victorian prudery – and the Cambridge Women's Training College, later to be known as Hughes Hall. Just prior to these women's colleges, in 1869, another new type of foundation came about in the form of the Non-Collegiate Students' Board, an institution set up specifically to cater for students who wanted to study at the university but could not afford membership of one of the wealthy, endowed colleges. This later became Fitzwilliam College.

Several theological colleges were established at Cambridge at this time, though only one of them was a full university foundation, Selwyn College of 1879. Finally, in the closing years of Victoria's long reign, two colleges migrated to Cambridge from elsewhere: Homerton, the local teachers' training college, from east London; and St Edmund's House (now St Edmund's College), originally a Roman Catholic lodging house which found its way to Cambridge via Douai in Flanders and Ware in Hertfordshire.

The nineteenth century at Cambridge was a period of unprecedented architectural development throughout the town, but particularly in the colleges and the university. The industrious Victorians built a phenomenal number of new buildings, expanding many college sites, but also sometimes restoring too severely, or completely demolishing older structures and superseding them with inferior replacements. With the introduction of many new subjects, in particular the practical natural sciences, the university had to expand its facilities considerably. New university sites began to spring up all over the town, with a particular concentration in the areas today known as the New Museums Site and the Downing Site, both in the southern quarter of the town centre. The design of many of these new buildings in Cambridge reflects the period's diverse tastes, and the town is a showcase for the work of these prolific designers, particularly George Gilbert Scott, Alfred Waterhouse (fig. 102) and Basil Champneys (figs 103–4). The town of today really started to take shape in the latter half of the nineteenth century.

101. The Fitzwilliam Museum, Trumpington Street (1837–75) by George Basevi. This architect was one of the most renowned pupils of Sir John Soane and, after leaving Soane's employ, he set out on a grand tour of Italy and Greece. His design for the museum is thought to have been inspired partly by the remains of a Roman building he came across at Brescia in 1820. The rich interior of the entrance hall is the work of C.R. Cockerell. Much has since been added to the south of Basevi's original building shown here.

101

102. The Waterhouse Building, Jesus College
(1869–70), by Alfred Waterhouse.

103 and *104.* Basil Champneys at Newnham
College: Clough Hall (1888) and Sidgwick Hall
(1880).

102

103

Modern Cambridge

In 1800 Cambridge town centre was surrounded by green fields, but by 1900 it was ringed by a multiplicity of houses. With the steady peripheral growth that had started after Enclosure, the gradual coalescence of the surrounding villages was inevitable, and the suburban sprawl slowly stretched out to the many village satellites that were only a mile or two away: Girton to the north; Chesterton, Fen Ditton and Cherry Hinton to the east; Trumpington and Shelford to the south; and Grantchester and Newnham to the south-west. However, the countryside still penetrated right into the town centre from the west, south and east, a characteristic of the city that has survived to the present day (figs 23, 144).

The expansion and development of Cambridge since the nineteenth century have followed a simple pattern: the university and colleges have built westwards, while the city has built to the north, east and south, and this still continues today. Before the Second World War, in the town centre itself, some of the colleges were responsible for a large amount of unfortunate demolition, mainly in the area of Magdalene and Bridge Streets around Magdalene and St John's Colleges, just as Henry VI had done at King's some five hundred years earlier. But the effect of the war, and the subsequent preservation of historic buildings, whether monumental or domestic, fortunately checked the earlier policy of fairly arbitrary destruction for purposes of expansion. This particular example, at Magdalene and St John's, illustrated how whole areas of the townscape could still be changed so easily for academic expansion, though this was to be the last instance on such a large scale. This northern area of the town centre, just below Castle Hill, had evolved with the original port in the days of the thriving river industry. It was a lively, busy district with rows of small-scale terraces dissected by narrow lanes and courtyards, from Northampton Street in the north to Bridge Street in the south. These two colleges needed to expand, and so began to demolish the 'slums' that surrounded them, mainly down the western side of Magdalene and Bridge Streets. Magdalene wanted to build a new court opposite the main college, and St John's a new court and car park along the strip of land to the east of its ancient buildings. Between them they cleared about a third of all the property in that area to create what at St John's turned out to be rather drab semi-modern buildings by Sir Edward Maufe. At Magdalene, however, the results were eventually more sympathetic, though only because of a temporary lack of funds, which slowed down building progress, and the intervention of the war. The ambitious scheme at Magdalene, by Sir Edwin Lutyens, of which only the west range was completed, would have resulted in the demolition of even more property. But, by the 1950s, when building was resumed, attitudes had changed, and the existing, older buildings were restored with a few additions to the same scale. However, this was not the end of it and in the 1960s much property on the east side of Bridge Street was demolished by the City Council in order to build the city's first multi-storey car park in Park Street. Had this whole area of the ancient city not been so savagely mutilated by the colleges and the City Council, it would have undoubtedly been an area of great charm, as can be imagined from the few surviving buildings (figs 105–6, 108).

As in every other English town or city, serious problems started in the 1920s, when the motor vehicle slowly began to intrude. The initial effects of this in Cambridge were that many of the narrow streets had to be widened: notably Jesus Lane in 1922, Bridge Street in 1938, Park Street in 1956, and Round Church Street in 1961. This, along with the demolition of some street façades, completely changed the character of many parts of the town. As for the town in general, it was soon decided that

Cambridge needed bigger and better shopping facilities, largely based on the American model, as was the trend throughout the country from the 1950s onwards. Here, Cambridge was particularly unlucky and suffered from two such developments. It was a curious and ironic fact in Cambridge that there had been an initial preference to leave the historic centre alone, and to place the new commercial development on the east side of town around Fitzroy and Burleigh Streets. This much loved area known locally as 'The Kite', was full of small-scale, nineteenth-century artisan terraces. Yet in the end Cambridge received both: the Lion Yard and Petty Cury shopping precinct right in its middle, and then the Grafton Centre was built wrecking the Kite area. A link between these two shopping havens had also been planned, via the park known as Christ's Pieces, and the now extremely tired-looking and dated Bradwells Court was prematurely built along this axis (1960–2), to lure the consumer from one to the other. The renewal of Bradwells Court is currently on the drawing board, long overdue, and the biggest yet shopping mall for Cambridge – The Grand Arcade – next to Lion Yard, is under construction and due to be completed in 2008. The trend continues and Cambridge has, like so many other towns, suffered the fate of modern consumerism and the uncontrollable force of contemporary shopping demands. Streets that not so long ago contained a variety of individual retailers, now follow the national template of endless chain-stores, international coffee shops, mobile phone shops and a glut of chain-restaurants and bars, so often bundled together in plastic arcades indistinguishable from one town to the next housed in sheds of ephemeral, transient architecture – the endless blight on historic town centres such as Cambridge.

105. Surviving timber framed buildings in the northern area of the city centre around Magdalene and Bridge Streets. St Clement's Church can be seen in the distance.

105

106

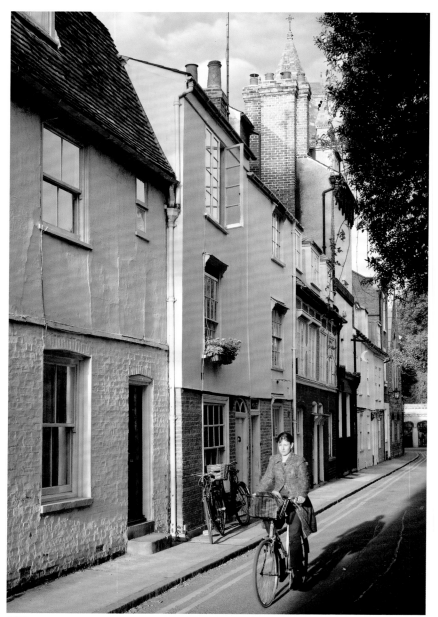

107

106. *Portugal Place, with the tower of St John's College Chapel.*

107. *Little Saint Mary's Lane.*

108. Surviving sixteenth- and seventeenth-century houses at the corner of Magdalene Street and Northampton Street.

109. Trinity Street, with the front of Whewell's Court (1859–68) by Anthony Salvin, Trinity College, and the Trinity Street Post Office with Heffers Booksellers beyond.

110. Oriel window at the Old Schools, Trinity Lane, with Trinity Hall to the right, and Clare College Chapel beyond.

109

Within the university, one of the most important inter-war events in Cambridge was the crossing of the river by Clare College to build Memorial Court on the west side of Queen's Road, thus initiating a new area of academic expansion, other than domestic housing. Clare did this largely in response to the increased number of students applying to universities after the First World War and, at the time, this decision to expand west of the river was heavily criticised. It was, however, the perfect solution to academic city centre congestion, and this was encouraged after the Second World War by the Cambridge planners, Holford and Wright, in 1950. Memorial Court was designed by Sir Giles Gilbert Scott and built between 1923 and 1934 in a neo-Georgian style on a large court plan open to the west. Before its completion, Scott was also employed by the university to design the new University Library which was built in 1931–4, directly on axis to the immediate west of Memorial Court (fig. 111). This massive brick building, with its tall central tower, has, like King's College Chapel,

become one of the dominant features of the Cambridge skyline (fig. 112).

This area to the west of Queen's Road started to develop into what was to become a secondary campus, and which today still continues to push westwards. Several new colleges were also founded in the post-war era, and all were built on this western side of the city: New Hall (1962–6, figs 113, 176), Churchill (1959–68, fig. 116), Darwin (1965–6, fig. 170), Clare Hall (1966–9, fig. 177), Lucy Cavendish (1970), Wolfson (1972–7, initially University College), Fitzwilliam (1961–7, fig. 115), and Robinson (1977–80, figs 178, 181–3).

Undoubtedly, it is the individual colleges who have, with a few exceptions, handled their modern development and expansion most successfully in Cambridge. By contrast, the standard of university development in the twentieth century was generally poor and unsympathetic to the townscape, as can be seen on a walk around the New Museums Site, the Downing Site, the Mill Lane Site or the Engineering Laboratories, all of which are just off the historic city centre.

111. Sir Giles Gilbert Scott at Clare College's Memorial Court (right) and the University Library (left). Memorial Court had the new college library boldly placed right in its middle in 1986 (by Sir Philip Dowson), breaking its central axis which previously gave a powerful vista in line with the tower of the University Library, shown here before extensive expansion to the west (left).

112. The University Library with the fields of west Cambridgeshire beyond, from the tower of St John's College Chapel.

111

112

The Sidgwick Site, between Sidgwick Avenue and West Road, with original buildings by Casson Conder & Partners, was an improvement on these, and now contains several representative buildings from the 1950s and the 1960s, most notably James Stirling's highly controversial History Faculty of 1964–8, referred to by Pevsner as 'anti-architecture' (fig. 114).

As with the modern shopping developments that were foisted on the town, the equally large university departments, such as the University Chemical Laboratory in Lensfield Road, would have been far better located outside the city centre. All of this twentieth-century development occupied prime city centre locations which should have been used for more appropriate purposes, such as housing, but instead there are now a mass of such monolithic buildings containing university departments that are all having to be re-organised owing to the phenomenal progress in modern technology, often dictating a new functional requirement for their needs. The Deer Report of 1965 recommended a move even further out to the open west field site for future university expansion, where such famous Cambridge

departments as the Cavendish Physics Laboratory was one of the first to relocate, taking advantage of room to breathe and expand in the future whenever necessary.

After half a century of debate concerning the future of Cambridge, involving many controversial decisions by the planners, the Cambridge Local Plan (2006) outlines future development and land use policy for the city, carefully preserving characteristics of its historical growth. Today, Cambridgeshire has one of the fastest growing economies and populations in the country, and the area around Cambridge itself has been labelled by the Government as part of the M11 Corridor, one of several large growth areas of substantial development. Previously, much of this growth was concentrated in the surrounding villages beyond the Green Belt, which resulted in a sharp rise in commuting by car into the city and all the concomitant congestion and pollution. A lack of space to build in the city itself, resulting in severely inflated property prices, also compounded these trends and forced people to live further afield in more affordable areas. Cambridge in fact has almost twice as

113. The entrance to New Hall, by Chamberlin, Powell and Bon, showing the 'orange peel' dome of this women's college. As with Basil Champneys' delightful interpretation for one of the first women's colleges at Cambridge in the late nineteenth century – with his decidedly feminine Queen Anne style at Newnham – so the designers here created these buildings also to exude a feminine aura, though in the more blatant era of the mid-1960s.

114. The History Faculty (1964–8) by James Stirling, probably the most controversial building of modern times in Cambridge. Comments at the time ranged from 'actively ugly' (Pevsner) to 'something rather strange and original' (Summerson) and 'visually striking, a great work of architecture' (Booth & Taylor). This was, indeed, a shock to the establishment at the time, but it was a building that made one think about what was going on within it, and it offered simple and satisfying explanations. Sadly, however, it has been constantly plagued by leaking roofs and peeling red tiles.

113

114

115. *The hall at Fitzwilliam College (1961–7) by Sir Denys Lasdun.*

116. Churchill College (1959–68), by Richard Sheppard, Robson & Partners.

many jobs as residents in work, and the latest prediction is that the city is set to grow rapidly over the next fifteen years by up to 30 per cent in population. The Structure Plan states that 12,500 new homes are to be created by 2016: 6,500 to be built in the urban area itself and the other 6,000 around the edge of the city on land to be released from the Green Belt. Extensive urban renewal on brown-field sites is already well underway, with many residential and commercial projects currently taking place, especially in the south of the city. This large and comparatively quick expansion will inevitably be reflected in a noticeable change in the physical environment. Tens of thousands of people will relocate here, along with many new businesses and other organisations, as a continuation of 'The Cambridge Phenomenon', which all began back in the 1970s. That initial influx of high-tech industry which developed in the city, via the university, gradually gave rise to the Cambridge Science Park, which has since been joined by many other similar developments.

This new expansion of Cambridge concentrates on six specific areas: **1.** The historic core and its immediately surrounding central zone will be enhanced, and priority given to the pedestrian with a progressive discouragement to the car. There will be a concerted effort to turn Cambridge into a 'sub-regional shopping destination' with its main attraction being the Grand Arcade shopping development on St Andrew's Street. **2.** The station area, south of the city centre, will be regenerated with much high-density residential and commercial development supporting a major improvement to the quality of the transport interchange. There are then four peripheral areas that will be concentrated on as a focus for future employment and residential expansion. **3.** In the north, a new railway station and transport interchange at Chesterton Sidings is planned. **4.** In the south, land is to be taken from the Green Belt to expand Addenbrooke's Hospital, and new residential communities will be created to

the east and south of Trumpington in support of this. **5.** On the east side of the city, Cambridge Airport will be relocated and that area used for high density mixed-use urban expansion. **6.** To the west, the university will continue to develop its west Cambridge site, not only for academic research and teaching purposes, but also for residential and sports facilities. When required in the future, land will also be allocated on the west side for university expansion between Madingley Road and the Huntingdon Road.

In all this peripheral development, major improvements are planned to the transport infrastructure of the city as a whole, to include high quality public transport. The report also states that there is an intention to enhance and improve the city's landscape structure, including the network of central parks and commons, the river valley and the green corridors that penetrate the city, as well as the landscape setting of the city edge. This is an ambitious plan and, if carried through successfully, the Cambridge of 2020 could be quite a different place to what it is today.

With regard to actual buildings in this grand plan, it will be fascinating to see what evolves. The last twenty years in Cambridge have seen many exciting new buildings, by both local and internationally renowned architects, ranging in style from Quinlan Terry at Downing College (fig. 117), through to Foster Associates at the Law Faculty (figs 122–3), and the Edward Cullinan Partnership at the Divinity School (fig. 124) and the Centre for Mathematical Sciences (fig. 125), with many others in between (figs 118–21). With the occasional exception – such as S&P's Parkside Swimming Pool (fig. 120) – it largely continues to be the wealthy colleges and the university who are able to direct considerable resources at their buildings to perpetuate the tradition of great architecture in this small city on the edge of the Fens.

117

118

117. *The Maitland Robinson Library, Downing College (1990–2), by Quinlan Terry.*

118. *The Judge Institute of Management Studies (conversion of Old Addenbrooke's Hospital, Trumpington Street, 1993–6) by John Outram Associates.*

119. *The Queen's Building, Emmanuel College (1995), by Michael Hopkins.*

120. *Parkside Swimming Pool (1999) by S&P Architects.*

121. *The Møller Centre, Churchill College (1992), by Henning Larsen.*

119

120

121

123

124

125

122 (left) and *123. The Law Faculty (1995) by Foster Associates.*

124. The Faculty of Divinity (2000) by the Edward Cullinan Partnership.

125. The Centre for Mathematical Sciences (2003) by the Edward Cullinan Partnership.

126. Cambridge city centre in late November.

126

127. The Pepys Building, Magdalene College (1587–1703), designer unknown, but central section possibly by Robert Hooke sometime between 1640 and 1679. The famous diarist Samuel Pepys bequeathed his library to the college in his will of 1703 and the books were installed in 1724.

128. Peterhouse Chapel (1628–32), designer unknown, but built during the mastership of Dr Matthew Wren, Christopher Wren's uncle. Originally a brick building, but later faced in stone, it is described by Nikolaus Pevsner as 'the most remarkable building of its date in Cambridge'.

129. *Spring punts at Trinity College.*

130. *Autumn along the Backs at Clare and King's Colleges.*

129

131. New Court and the Bridge of Sighs, St John's College (1826–31), by Rickman & Hutchinson.

131

132

132. *Golden dragon, King's College Chapel.*

133. *Keystone angel, Westminster College.*

133

134

134 and *135*. Punts at Trinity College.

135

136. *King's College Bridge and Bodley's Court.*

136

137

139. Reunion dinner, St John's College hall (1511–20) by William Swayne.

140

140. Ready for dinner, King's College hall (1824–8) by William Wilkins.

141. Old Hall gable, Newnham College (1875) by Basil Champneys.

142. The American Cemetery at Madingley. The site of the World War II Cambridge American Cemetery and Memorial, on the west side of the city, was donated by the university. Just over thirty acres in size, it contains 3,812 graves of American military personnel. The Wall of the Missing, which runs along the south side of the site, contains a further 5,126 names of Americans who gave their lives in the service of their country, but who were never recovered or identified. Lying on a northern slope, the cemetery is beautifully planted and tended, with many glorious tree colours in the autumn.

141

143. *Frozen tree, Bodley's Court, King's College.*

THE EVOLVING COLLEGE PLAN

The evolution of the Cambridge colleges has produced one of the most remarkable series of buildings in English architecture. From the hall at Peterhouse of 1286 (fig. 33), the first college building, through to the most recent complete foundation, Robinson College of the late 1970s (figs 178, 181–3), seven centuries of fascinating growth have taken place and it is, essentially, these foundations that have created the unique Cambridge townscape.

There appears to have been no organised plan or system of building for the earliest colleges at Cambridge. A founder would simply purchase a site on which there were adequate buildings to house his scholars and, as funds became available, new land and buildings would be added. The basic requirements in the earliest foundations were rooms for the Fellows to sleep and study, a kitchen, a dining room and an office. As the religious needs of the community were catered for by the nearest parish church, a chapel was unnecessary. The library was simply a chest in the strong room in which books were kept, and the Master of the college occupied an ordinary chamber like everyone else. The process of growth in these early foundations was very slow, and none of the founders lived to see the completion of their colleges. As this random development progressed, the other component buildings that so characterise a college today – hall, chapel, library, Master's Lodge and gatehouse – were gradually introduced. The attempt to create such an organised layout was not undertaken until long after the establishment of these earliest colleges.

During the mid-fourteenth century an organised plan began to evolve, and colleges started to form self-contained communities set up along the lines of a monastery, the analogy being obvious in the basic plan form of the rectilinear courtyard – termed the 'court' at Cambridge and the 'quad'

at Oxford. Certain buildings used features clearly taken from monastic architecture: the cloister; the refectory, with its kitchen and offices; the chapel, and the Master's Lodge.

The evolving college plan at Cambridge can be divided into nine phases, although its basic form had taken shape by the end of the fourteenth century. Thereafter, variations followed, with different planning ideas modifying or improving on the theme.

1. Random Building

When the first group of colleges were founded in the thirteenth and fourteenth centuries, only random building took place, in a piecemeal, disorganised fashion with no overall plan in mind. When the founder of Peterhouse, Hugh de Balsham, died in 1286, six years after establishing the college, he left his fifteen scholars 300 marks to erect new buildings. They used this to enlarge the site and built the hall, but the main court was not begun until the second half of the fifteenth century. At Hervey de Stanton's foundation, Michaelhouse (later part of Trinity), he, and then his executors, simply acquired connecting properties over a number of years in which gradually to increase and house the college members. The original buildings of Clare Hall (now Clare College), built by the Countess of Clare after 1338, were destroyed by fire in the early 1500s but, as far as is known, they were not built on a quadrangular plan. Edward III's scholars at King's Hall (later also part of Trinity), lived in the house of Robert de Croyland and, although it was largely rebuilt and adapted for them in the late fourteenth century, it was not arranged on a quadrangular layout either until 1420.

144 (left). Aerial view of Cambridge city centre from the south showing the typical courtyard layouts of many of the older colleges.

145

145. Chapel lantern, Pembroke College (1663–5), by Sir Christopher Wren.

146

146. Chapel lantern, Emmanuel College (1668–74), by Sir Christopher Wren.

147. The fountain (1601–15) and gatehouse (1518–35), Trinity College.

148. New Court cloister and herbaceous border, St John's College.

149. St John's Street, with Trinity College Chapel and the gatehouse and chapel at St John's College.

2. The Early Courts

In quick succession, between 1347 and 1352, the second group of colleges was established (see p. 188) and among these are to be found the first enclosed courtyards at Cambridge.

The small Old Court at Pembroke College (fig. 150) was the first court at Cambridge to contain all of the buildings required for college life, including a chapel as part of its original composition. Its dates are uncertain, but building began in the late 1340s and continued well into the fifteenth century. Unfortunately, the south and east ranges were demolished by the Victorians, and prior to that the whole court was ashlared in the early eighteenth century, thus Italianising and covering over the original brick façades (fig. 74).

Little remains of the original architecture of Gonville Hall (now Gonville & Caius College), though this was also an early quadrangular composition. The Old, or Principal Court, at Trinity Hall was built in 1350–74 and was the largest enclosed plan to that date, measuring 115 x 80 feet. But the most intact example of a medieval court in Cambridge is Old Court at Corpus Christi (fig. 151). This was built in 1352–77 and, with its simple, carefully planned

150. The original layout of Pembroke College as shown in David Loggan's illustration of c.1675. This is one of a series of wonderful drawings by Loggan that shows Cambridge compositions largely in their original states, long before the Victorian demolition squads came along. Here, at Pembroke, one can see the medieval intimacy of the original courtyard layouts, but in the 1870s Alfred Waterhouse was employed to demolish the dividing range and the east range, which he replaced with the existing hall. Waterhouse also built Red Buildings and the library at that time, both south of Wren's chapel, which can be seen here as the then southernmost range of the whole composition, only newly completed about ten years before Loggan's engraving.

150

arrangement of parts, is regarded as the first completely enclosed composition on the court plan. Apart from the west half of the south range, which was rebuilt in 1823–7, the buildings are virtually unchanged but for the buttresses, which were added between 1487 and 1515. The plan here originally consisted of hall, kitchens, and Master's Lodge in the south range, with chambers in all the other three sides. It did not, however, have a chapel, and St Bene't's Church, to the immediate north-east, served as such.

Thus, the very gradual synthesis of the basic college plan took shape in the third quarter of the fourteenth century. The next major step was taken at Oxford by William of Wykeham, with his own innovatory designs for New College in 1379. Wykeham possessed considerable building knowledge having been clerk of works to Edward III. It was then that students for the first time were to live with their teachers, and the college community thus became an educational establishment, as opposed to a brotherhood of Fellows.

151. Old Court at Corpus Christi College, showing the north range with the tower of St Bene't's Church behind. The court remains almost intact, apart from the west half of the south range which was rebuilt in 1823–7 when William Wilkins built New Court next door (fig. 92). The north side of the north range is best preserved, with a gallery connecting the court to the church, added in c.1500.

151

152. King's Parade, showing the magnificent Perpendicular Gothic college chapel (1446–1515) and the nineteenth-century Gothic Revival gatehouse and screen (1824–8). The building to the right is the east range of the university's Old Schools complex.

152

153. *String quartet at Magdalene College May Ball.*

154

154. Night punting at Trinity College May Ball.

3. The Organised Quadrangle after Wykeham at Oxford (1380–6)

Wykeham possessed considerable building knowledge, as he had been Clerk of Works to Edward III, and he himself undertook the design of his college, using his predecessors as a guide. He completed the college in six years without interruption, and in doing so produced the first example of a totally organised plan containing all of the principal elements of collegiate architecture: hall, library, Master's lodge, chapel, chambers, and even a towered gatehouse, the first occurrence of that feature within the college composition. Great Quad, at New College, was built to a clear and logically worked-out plan, and Wykeham's ideas provided either the model or inspiration for most of the succeeding foundations at Oxford, new colleges being planned, or existing ones converted. It is from this point that organised collegiate architecture really begins.

At first, Cambridge was little affected by Wykeham's innovations, and it was over half a century before his influence was felt here when, in 1441, Henry VI founded King's College. Henry's own design for King's, from his 'wille and entent' of 1448, was based on Wykeham's large enclosed quad, but his deposition and death meant that he was unable to complete his ideas, and only the famous chapel was built as the north side of the intended plan.

4. The College Court as a Derivative of the Medieval Manor House

The Old Court at Queens' College (figs. 155–6 and 158) was designed and built by Reginald Ely, the King's mason in 1448–9, and was the first complete college court containing all the principal elements to be built at Cambridge in one go

without interruption. Professor Willis (in his *Architectural History of the University of Cambridge*, 1886) pointed out an interesting similarity between the ground plan of the two oldest courts at Queens' College to that of Haddon Hall in Derbyshire. That medieval manor house slightly pre-dates Queens' and, with the exception of a few minor points, the overall arrangement of the buildings in the two compositions is almost identical. This, and other examples, led Willis to put forward a theory that the great country manor houses of the fifteenth century also played an important role in the planning of the medieval college.

In the typical plan of the early colleges the main court would have one side ranged along the public street (normally the east or west side), through the centre of which would be the main entrance via a turreted gatehouse. This layout has given rise to one of the most striking and charming characteristics of the Cambridge townscape – small entrances opening into the tranquil atmosphere of beautiful courtyards. On entering the courtyard through the gatehouse, the hall would normally be facing in the opposite range, thus remote from the street. The kitchen and buttery (store rooms) would be part of the hall range, and would be placed in the corner of the court so that they did not look inward, but were lit and ventilated to the outer court side. As the plan form progressed, the buttery and kitchen would later be separated from the hall by the 'screens passage', providing access to a second court (Queens' was the first to devise such a plan and build a second court, fig. 157). The Master's Lodge and Fellows' Combination Room would normally connect with the opposite end of the hall range, providing the Master and/or Fellows with direct access for dining. As chapels are laid out on an east–west axis, they had to be located in either the north or south range, and the north was normally chosen, reserving the warmer south range for chambers. Chambers would thus occupy most of the south and east sides, and whatever space remained in the other ranges. The chambers themselves would normally be arranged in vertical stacks located off staircases, a tradition that has predominated. The library was randomly placed, and would usually be at first floor level.

The college precinct was not restricted solely to the buildings of the courtyard and, once the collegiate system had been established, it was intended that not only the academic but also the recreational needs of the community should be met within the confines of the college grounds. In particular, the gardens became of paramount importance as a desirable adjunct to intellectual college life.

155

156

155 and 156. Old Court at Queens' College, the west and north ranges, and the east range with the gatehouse (all 1448–9). The buildings are brick faced over a clunch limestone core, and the architect is thought to have been the local master mason, Reginald Ely, who was also responsible for much of the work at King's College Chapel. The north half of the west range contains the hall, which has a richly decorated nineteenth-century interior by the Arts & Crafts firm of Morris & Co.

157

157. The President's Lodge at Queens' College (c.1540), forming the north range of Cloister Court, referred to by Pevsner as 'one of the most picturesque of English timber framed structures, its beauty being one of irregularity and happy accident rather than plan'.

158. The east elevation of Queens' College Old Court on Queens' Lane, photographed from the Master's Lodge at St Catharine's College.

158

5. The Three-Sided, or 'Sanitary' Plan, after Dr Caius (1565–9)

The effect of the Reformation on collegiate architecture is more marked in elevation than in plan, owing to the stylistic changes which accompanied it as English art and architecture began to be influenced by the Italian Renaissance. But during this exciting period a new plan form was also introduced by an eminent physician and amateur architect, Dr John Caius (pronounced 'Keys' – he Latinised his name, as was the fashion of the time).

The young Caius entered Gonville Hall as a scholar in 1529, later to become a Fellow between 1533 and 1545, during which time he also studied medicine at Padua and undertook a grand tour, travelling widely through Europe. Upon his return to England Caius rose quickly in his profession, becoming personal physician to both Edward VI and 'Bloody' Queen Mary. In 1557 he refounded Gonville Hall, and enjoyed the unique position in the history of Cambridge colleges of being both Founder and Master of the new college, Gonville & Caius. In 1565 he set about adding a new court to the original foundation, Caius Court (fig. 159), but this was only to have buildings on three sides: the existing south range of Gonville Hall (now Gonville Court) provided the north side, and Caius built two new ranges as the east and west sides, but only a wall with a gate closed off the south side. This new, three-sided composition, has also been termed the 'sanitary plan', as it was deliberately designed

159. Caius Court at Gonville & Caius College – an open, three-sided composition thought up and designed by Dr John Caius as a way of letting fresh air enter and circulate for the health benefits of those within. Caius built the two flanking ranges here, as the east and west sides, with the south range of the older Gonville Court forming the north side, and only a wall, with the Gate of Honour, closing the court to the south. The grand, classical buildings beyond are the Senate House to the left, and the Old University Library to the right, now the library of the college.

159

to aid health and hygiene, as a clause in Caius's refoundation statutes stated:

> We decree that no building be constructed which shall shut in the entire south side of the college of our foundation, lest for lack of free ventilation the air should become foul, the health of our college, and still more the health of Gonville's college, should become impaired and disease and death be thereby rendered more frequent in both.

Caius was not completely innovative in this new composition, as it was a scheme often used in the layout of French country houses, which he may well have observed during his travels. Nevertheless, his idea was influential and this new plan form became widely adopted at Cambridge in place of the completely enclosed court common before the Reformation, although more for reasons of creative composition than for the alleviation of disease and death.

In the early seventeenth century an interesting modification was made to the three-sided plan at Cambridge when the chapel at Peterhouse was placed in the centre of the open east end of Old Court, joined to the flanking north and south ranges only by an open arcade with a gallery above, still providing good 'ventilation' to the court. The same device was employed at Emmanuel by Wren in the late 1660s (figs 63, 69).

The idea of the three-sided plan thus broke with the medieval tradition of the completely enclosed courtyard, and it introduced a new concept of space into college planning, creating a relationship between the inner court and the outer surroundings – between private and public – while still retaining boundaries. However, between the Restoration and the nineteenth century there was a predominant return to the enclosed quadrangular plan.

6. Downing College and the Campus Plan (1807–20)

It was not until the early 1800s, when the local architect, William Wilkins, built Downing College, that the next major development took place. In its layout Downing was completely revolutionary as it was designed on the idea of a spacious campus, as opposed to an enclosed courtyard. This was the first example of this new type of composition in collegiate planning, preceding Thomas Jefferson's University of Virginia, at Charlottesville, USA, by ten years. Unfortunately, Wilkins was not able to complete his ideas for Downing in full, but his intended plan placed individual blocks of buildings set as broken ranges and forming a court measuring 350 × 300 feet, roughly equal in area today to the largest court in Cambridge, Great Court at Trinity. This expansive composition was to be entered from Downing Street through a Greek Doric propylaeum. The east and west ranges were each composed of two separated blocks of chambers to north and south, with a house disposed between them: on the east side was the house of the professor of medicine, and on the west the professor of law. At the southern end of the east range was the similarly free-standing Master's Lodge, and on the west range the hall, each with Ionic porticos on the south and court elevations, intended to match those of the south range, containing the library and chapel, but which was never built.

Wilkins' ideas at Downing were stunning, and they made a complete break with the traditional monastic courtyard. The whole feel of this new college was to be one of space, with buildings set in a landscape that could flow freely between them, and the most notable difference in the plan to that of its predecessors – quite apart from the immense scale – was that all of the buildings were designed as individual and separated units. Sadly, however, only the east and west sides were built, and they were later adapted to form

160. St. Catharine's College (1673–1704) by Robert Grumbold.

161

161. The hall at Magdalene College (1519).

162 (previous page). *City centre in snow.*

163. *The Countess of Shrewsbury,
The Shrewsbury Tower, St John's College.*

164. *Sir Isaac Newton by Roubiliac (1755),
the antechapel, Trinity College.*

163

QUAM IN
P H PINCKNEY
N L J PISANI
C D PITMAN
R W PORRITT
L J PORTER
J H C POWELL
H G PRESTON
R M PROCTER
J A PRYCE
A S PRYOR
D J RAMSAY
J H L SINCLAIR
G DE T SKIPWITH
B A SMITH
H W SMITH
J C SMITH
R A L SMITH
R M C SOMERVELL
G H B SOWTER
W B STANHOPE-LOVELL
R H STEVENS
R J P STEWART
W A M B STEWART
H J STIRLING
R F STOREY
J M STRANG STEEL
J G STRUTHERS
M STRUTT
A J STUART
VISCOUNT STUART
J A SWANN
G H SWIFT
M SWITHINBANK
J D A SYRETT
C G TANNER
E J TARRANT
J R N TAYLOR
T J TAYLOR
W TAYLOR-YOUNG
C J TENNYSON
I B TETLEY
J D A THARP
A E THICKETT
P M H THOMAS
G THOMERSON
D S THOMSON
F B THORPE
B K F TIGHE
P R TOMKIN
J E O TREHERNE

165. *The east range of Downing College (1807–13) by William Wilkins. This eastern line of buildings originally consisted of the Master's Lodge to the south and the house of the professor of medicine in the middle with a block of chambers to either side of it, all of which are clearly demarked here sitting forward of the later connections which were added by E.M. Barry in 1873–6. The same layout was repeated on the opposite side of the enormous court, with the hall facing the Master's Lodge and the professor of law facing the professor of medicine. The separate buildings of the west range were also connected by Barry in the 1870s.*

continuous ranges, thus changing the original concept of the designer. Nevertheless, enough was built to give an impression of the desired effect and, regardless of the changes, Downing remains a surprise to visitors to Cambridge who, upon completion of the standard tour of the older colleges, find themselves in this large open court surrounded by low neo-Classical ranges (fig. 165).

7. The Nineteenth and Twentieth Centuries

The nineteenth century saw a very considerable amount of building activity in Cambridge, though no attempt was made to follow Wilkins in either plan or style. Many new buildings were added to existing colleges and many new courts created, both on the enclosed and three-sided plan. The Victorians demolished much, and two of the greatest losses were at Pembroke and St John's. At Pembroke, the east and south ranges of the early medieval Old Court were pulled down (fig. 150), and the new hall, by Alfred Waterhouse, inserted in place of the east range. At St John's, in order to make way for a new, much larger chapel by George Gilbert Scott (fig. 166), its thirteenth-century predecessor was destroyed, thus sacrificing the medieval plan and intimate character of that college's First Court (fig. 167). These were the most regrettable instances of Victorian vandalism at Cambridge.

It is curious that at this time, with the introduction of the first women's colleges (Newnham, Girton and Hughes Hall), an

165

innovation in internal planning was also made. The architect at Girton was Alfred Waterhouse and, although he followed tradition in most of his design, he broke with the established pattern of rooms arranged on a vertical stack accessible from staircases, as in the older men's colleges, and instead introduced the corridor plan, which was also adopted at Newnham and Hughes Hall. Interestingly, almost all of the women's colleges founded in Oxford, a few years later than those in Cambridge, also employed the corridor plan instead of staircases.

Both Girton and Newnham were located in extensive grounds and their buildings were planned in a relatively free manner, allowing for easy future addition. Girton is composed of both enclosed and three-sided courts, while Newnham could be regarded as one large three-sided composition, its buildings following the site perimeter along Sidgwick Avenue and Grange Road, looking inwards to beautiful gardens with playing fields beyond.

The twentieth century was also a time of great expansion in most of the colleges, largely along traditional lines in planning terms until well after the Second World War. An exception to this, and a rather odd curiosity in terms of

collegiate development, was the Fisher Building at Queens' College of 1935–6 by Norman Drinkwater. This building extended Queens' site on to the west bank of the Cam and was most unusual in its curvilinear plan. This form may have seemed appropriate in one respect, in that it followed the contours of the site boundary (the small tributary of the river to its west, and Silver Street to the south), but it was

166. *St John's College Chapel (1863–9) by George Gilbert Scott and,* 167, *the original lay-out of the college, as illustrated by David Loggan in c.1675, showing the medieval chapel as the north range of First Court. Here, the wonderful homogeneity of plan and scale was lost at St John's, where previously the progression of the three stunning brick courtyards was superb.*

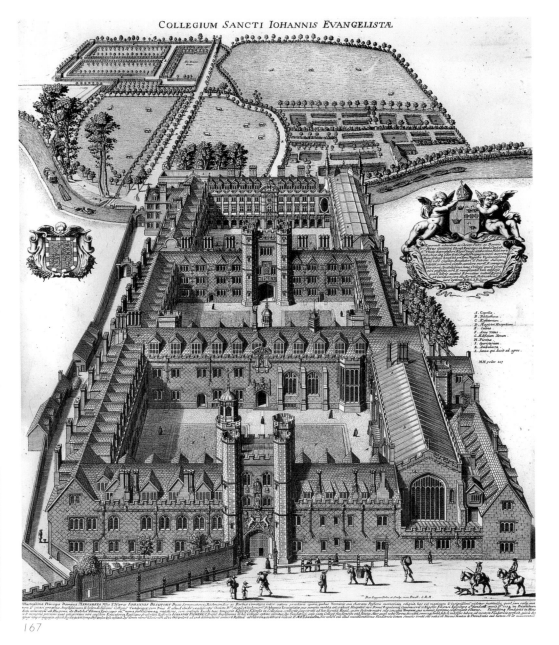

COLLEGIUM SANCTI IOHANNIS EVANGELISTÆ.

166

167

168. *The Senior Combination Room, Downing College (1966–70), by Howell, Killick, Partridge & Amis. One of the most satisfyingly successful modern buildings in Cambridge, illustrating how the reinterpretation of classical architecture, skilfully handled, is preferable to a solution of pastiche or reproduction. Here, this wonderful little pavilion sits comfortably in line with the neighbouring Greek Revival hall and Master's Lodge of almost 200 years earlier.*

169. *The Master's Lodge, Downing College (1807–13), by William Wilkins, and the spire of Our Lady and the English Martyrs (1885–90) by Dunn & Hansom.*

170. *The Old Granary, Darwin College. Darwin is a graduate college created in 1965 by three other colleges: Gonville & Caius, St John's and Trinity. It occupies a group of nineteenth-century buildings in Silver Street, on the west side of the river, most notably Newnham Grange, the Old Granary and the Hermitage, along with modern buildings added since.*

171. The Chancellor's Centre, Wolfson College (2003–4), by Brewer Smith & Brewer.

inevitably going to be unsympathetic to the addition of later buildings in that area and, particularly, to the formation of any court layout. This was something that would normally be taken into consideration when planning any new building in a college – that it could lend itself to future addition – but here it proved to be extremely difficult, as shown by the awkward juxtaposition which later arose with the building of Cripps Court in 1972–80 by Powell & Moya (fig. 172).

Throughout the 1960s and 1970s a massive acceleration in college building took place, unprecedented in the history of the town. Ten new colleges were founded, and many new additions were made to existing colleges creating new courts. In planning terms the most interesting of these additions were Harvey Court on West Road by Martin & Wilson, for Gonville & Caius College (1960–2), with its raised inner plinth over communal rooms, surrounded by

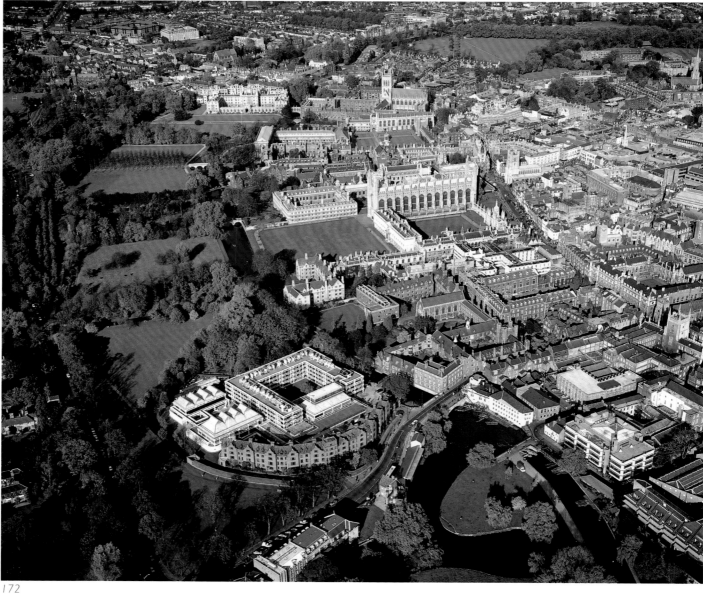

172. The Fisher Building and Cripps Court, Queens' College, are seen here in the foreground within the context of old Cambridge, surrounded by courtyards that grew and expanded from a simple, progressive planning policy. By contrast, the curvilinear form of Fisher was unsympathetic to future addition.

172

tiered, inward-looking living quarters fronted with terraces; the wonderful meandering plan of the Cripps Building at St John's of 1963–7 by Powell & Moya, which tied together the two halves of that college's west bank site; the joint undertaking of King's and St Catharine's colleges in the King's Lane Courts, a very clever piece of jigsaw-puzzle planning creating several new courts on the cramped city centre site of the colleges' adjoining borders; and Newnham College's Strachey Building, the first example in Cambridge of a Y-shaped plan.

Of the completely new foundations, two in particular are important with regard to the development of the college plan: Churchill and Robinson.

8. Churchill College – Courts within a Campus (1959–68)

At Churchill (fig. 173), Richard Sheppard's fascinating plan consists of a main primary court formed by surrounding secondary courts, the whole of which is set in a campus-like environment. This creative idea combined the traditional, monastic origins of Cambridge college planning with the innovative use of space used by Wilkins at Downing. The ten outer residential courts at Churchill are set in clusters within the landscape and, in effect, surround the main block of communal buildings. Instead of the traditional ranges forming each side of a court, a series of satellites encircle the heart, and the landscape, which flows freely between the individual

173. Churchill College from the west. As at Downing, the planning concept at Churchill was one of buildings set within a landscape, with space flowing freely around the individual components of the overall plan, though here those components were themselves ten small residential courtyards all set around the main cluster of communal buildings and, in effect, creating one large semi-enclosed space. This view shows three of the outer courts, to left and right, with the communal buildings in the middle distance. Above the treeline can be seen the University Library tower to the right, King's College Chapel in the middle, and St John's College Chapel to the left.

173

174. *The Jerwood Library, Trinity Hall (1998), by Freeland Rees Roberts.*

175

175. The river front, Old Court, Clare College (1640–1715), by Thomas and Robert Grumbold.

elements, becomes an integral part of the whole composition. Although this was a most imaginative reinterpretation of traditional ideas, opinions differed at the time as to whether such an open composition could succeed in representing the 'college' as a corporate institution. Now, almost half a century on, community life at Churchill has proven as successful as its enduring architecture, and it is one of the most satisfying modern developments in Cambridge from this period.

Churchill's collegiate neighbours in this area of west and north Cambridge, from the same period, were also interesting in their planning concepts. Peter Chamberlin's ingenious handling of internal space at New Hall, and his strong vistas in which water, gardens and sunken courts interacted with the architecture were, like Churchill, a vibrant new approach to college living (fig. 176). Sir Denys Lasdun's Fitzwilliam College, next door to New Hall, was similarly inventive, based upon the spiral, or 'snail shell' idea, with plenty of capacity for future growth as funds became available and, indeed, both of these colleges have recently expanded their sites considerably.

The 1960s at Cambridge also saw a growing need for more graduate accommodation to house the steadily increasing number of research students wanting to use the facilities offered by the university. Of the three graduate colleges that were founded (all in 1965), the most interesting architecturally was Clare Hall (fig. 177), by the Anglo-Swedish architect Ralph Erskine. This small-scale complex is a collection of individual houses and flats with accompanying communal rooms, and was designed to accommodate visiting academics and their families. The character of the whole composition, with a variety of open internal routes and spaces, is deliberately very domestic, the court in this instance being used more as a back yard for the houses, or as a pleasant atrium onto which many of the surrounding communal and study rooms open. Here, Erskine employed the enclosed plan in a completely different manner, and on a modest scale, far more intimate than the smallest of its Cambridge ancestors. From the domestic intimacy of Erskine at Clare Hall, the next phase in college planning at Cambridge went to the other extreme, with the building of the last college in this extraordinary seven-hundred-year story.

176. The sunken court with the Library, New Hall (1962–6).

177. Clare Hall (1966–9) by Ralph Erskine – an interwoven collection of domestic-scale buildings, courtyards and patios.

176

177

9. Robinson College – Courts within a Castle Bailey (1977–80)

Robinson was the first Cambridge college to be conceived for both men and women, and also to be designed with the dual function of being a college during the academic year and a conference centre during vacations. The choice of the 12.5 acre site in leafy west Cambridge met with severe opposition as it was an area zoned for residential use, but the trustees got their way and a design competition involving ten practices was undertaken, with the Glasgow firm of Gillespie, Kidd & Coia winning. It is particularly interesting here to compare the different approaches of the three runners-up with that of the winning scheme.

The site along Grange Road (between Herschel and Adams Roads) consisted of large nineteenth-century houses and their gardens, and is crossed by Bin Brook, a small tributary of the Cam. This delightful environment was, of course, a main dictating factor for the designers, and all three of the runners-up responded to it in a very similar manner: buildings dispersed widely throughout the whole area in a sensitive response to it and the surrounding locality. The scheme by MacCormac and Jamieson, in particular, proposed a series of twenty-one linked cruciform pavilions between which courts and partial courts were formed, the planning grid being so designed that it related to the pattern of the existing trees and created a collection of buildings as an integral part of the landscape. This was clearly a measured approach to the overall area, and it would have been an appropriate solution to college expansion in west Cambridge. In contrast, the winning plan concentrated the buildings around the eastern perimeter of the site abutting Grange Road, in the form of a massive double wall presenting the lower of its ranges to the public street, and a cliff-like façade to the undisturbed garden area to the west. The courts of the college are contained between these two vertical

accents as a long and continuous space and, if the eventual completion of the whole composition is ever achieved, the overall form will be one enormous three-sided court open towards the gardens.

This design at Robinson perpetuated traditional collegiate planning at Cambridge and continued the age-old separation of Town and Gown, though over the last twenty-five years excellent planting has softened the initial shock to the streetscape. The designers drew on many traditional sources: the placing of the main façade along the public street, with the calm and private college gardens behind; rooms laid out on the staircase plan, and all the necessary component parts in place and accessible from interconnecting communal spaces. However, the built form, and the attempt of the architects to re-interpret the 'generic college image', resulted in something quite different: a fortress-like monumentality throughout, reminiscent of a castle; the

178

178. The castle-like gatehouse of Robinson College, with its ramp approach.

179. Cambridge University Botanic Garden opened in 1846 on the new Bateman Street/Trumpington Road site at the instigation of the professor of botany, J.S. Henslow, who was Charles Darwin's teacher. Initially only twenty acres of the forty-acre site were planted, and the other twenty let out as allotments. The old, smaller Botanic Garden of around five acres was situated in the area of what is now the New Museums Site in the centre of town.

180. Clare College river front from the Fellows' Garden on the west bank, one of the most beautiful gardens in Cambridge.

179

entrance at a corner, with its ramp approach and portcullis-like screen (fig. 178); and perhaps the most noticeable innovation of all, the undefined inner spaces which resemble streets rather than courts (figs 181–2).

In the desire to achieve privacy for the college's inner sanctum from the outside world an extreme overstatement was achieved at Robinson. On the street side its defensive nature is almost offensive to the public, and on the private side the buildings fail to relate to the landscape in the traditional manner, but compete with and dominate it. The massive six-storey block of the main building forms a barrier making access to the gardens from the inner 'bailey' (the courts) of the 'castle' most awkward. Although some critics praised this plan as a sympathetic response to the site, it can also be seen as a rather drastic solution resulting in the subordination of the gardens to the gigantic wall (fig. 183). In this instance, the buildings and gardens have become two very separate elements, whereas traditionally they were treated integrally.

Over many centuries a relationship between Cambridge colleges and their surroundings has successfully evolved in both plan and scale, and in most instances a satisfactory harmony has been achieved. It is this homogeneity which has led, in part, to the unique quality of Cambridge townscape. In contemporary building, however, there have been a few highly controversial schemes, such as Denys Lasdun's New Court for Christ's College, which turned its overscaled back on the public elevation to King Street. Whereas that highly imaginative building was deemed most desirable by the college and was undoubtedly a great addition to the site, from the public viewpoint of the street it was not. The same was true of Robinson, which was equally regarded as an appropriate solution by its commissioning panel, though at the time not by the residents of leafy west Cambridge. But now, decades on, these two particular monolithic structures have integrated well and have become part of the accepted fabric of the modern city. Great architecture is often the result of imperiousness, and where this has

181. The street-like form of Long Court, Robinson College.

182. Front Court at Robinson, with the chapel and library.

181

182

occurred successfully at Cambridge — for instance, at King's College Chapel and in the many older colleges dominating street fronts — those buildings play an essential role within the overall composition of the town, creating a character that is the enduring essence of this place.

183. Robinson College and its garden. The hall and residential terraces of the college form a massive wall that subordinates the garden to that of a moat below the castle.

183

184. View from Garret Hostel Bridge across
Trinity Hall towards Clare and King's Colleges.

184

185. Winter painter.

186. Cows grazing on Scholars' Piece, King's College water meadow.

185

187

187. May Ball Marquee, King's College (1983 – The Stranglers were playing Golden Brown*).*

188. Pembroke College Chapel (1663–5) by Sir Christopher Wren.

188

189. *Bookseller, St Edward's Passage.*

190 *(right). The Eagle, an old coaching inn, Bene't Street.*

Date: 1280
Foundation: PETERHOUSE
Founder: Hugh de Balsham, Bishop of Ely
Location: Trumpington Street (G6)

Date: 1441
Foundation: KING'S COLLEGE
Founder: King Henry VI
Location: King's Parade (F5)

Date: 1317:1324: 1337: 1546
Foundation: TRINITY COLLEGE
Founder: King Henry VIII
Location: Trinity Street (F4)

Date: 1446: 1448: 1465
Foundation: QUEENS' COLLEGE
Founders: Margaret of Anjou & Eliz. Woodville
Location: Queens' Lane/Silver Street (F6)

Date: 1326: 1338: 1856
Foundation: CLARE COLLEGE
Founder: The Countess of Clare
Location: Trinity Lane (F5)

Date: 1473
Foundation: ST CATHARINE'S COLLEGE
Founder: Robert Woodlark
Location: Trumpington Street (FG6)

Date: 1347
Foundation: PEMBROKE COLLEGE
Founder: The Countess of Pembroke
Location: Trumpington Street (G6)

Date: 1496
Foundation: JESUS COLLEGE
Founder: John Alcock, Bishop of Ely
Location: Jesus Lane (H3-4)

Date: 1348: 1557
Foundation: GONVILLE & CAIUS
Founders: Edmund Gonville & John Caius
Location: Trinity Street (FG4-5)

Date: 1511
Foundation: ST JOHN'S COLLEGE
Founder: Lady Margaret Beaufort
Location: St John's Street (FG4)

Date: 1350
Foundation: TRINITY HALL
Founder: William Bateman, Bp of Norwich
Location: Trinity Lane (F5)

Date: 1584
Foundation: EMMANUEL COLLEGE
Founder: Sir Walter Mildmay
Location: St Andrew's Street (H5)

Date: 1352
Foundation: CORPUS CHRISTI COLLEGE
Founders: Guilds of Corpus Christi & St Mary
Location: Trumpington Street (G5-6)

Date: 1473
Foundation: SIDNEY SUSSEX COLLEGE
Founder: Lady Frances Sidney
Location: Sidney Street (G4)

Date: 1428: 1542
Foundation: MAGDALENE COLLEGE
Founder: Thomas, Lord Audley of Walden
Location: Magdalene Street (F3)

Date: 1800
Foundation: DOWNING COLLEGE
Founder: Sir George Downing III
Location: Regent Street (H6-7)

Date: 1437: 1505
Foundation: CHRIST'S COLLEGE
Founder: Lady Margaret Beaufort
Location: St Andrew's Street (H4-5)

Date: 1869: 1874: 1966
Foundation: FITZWILLIAM COLLEGE
Founder: Non-Collegiate Students' Board
Location: Huntingdon Rd/Storey's Way (D1-2)

Date: 1871

Foundation: NEWNHAM COLLEGE

Founder: Council for High. Ed. for Women

Location: Sidgwick Avenue *(DE7)*

Date: 1869: **1873**

Foundation: GIRTON COLLEGE

Founder: Emily Davies

Location: Huntingdon Road *(N. Cambridge)*

Date: 1879

Foundation: SELWYN COLLEGE

Founder: by committee (aft. Bishop Selwyn)

Location: Grange Road *(D6)*

Date: 1885: **1949**

Foundation: HUGHES HALL

Founder: Miss Clough (aft. Miss E.P. Hughes)

Location: Wollaston Road (off Mill Rd. - *J6*)

Date: 1894

Foundation: HOMERTON COLLEGE

Founder: Congregational Churches

Location: Hills Road *(K11)*

Date: 1896

Foundation: ST EDMUND'S COLLEGE

Founders: Duke of Norfolk & Baron von Hügel

Location: Mount Pleasant *(E2)*

Date: 1951: **1965**

Foundation: LUCY CAVENDISH COLLEGE

Founders: Bidder/Braithwaite/Wood-Legh

Location: Lady Margaret Road *(E3)*

Date: 1954

Foundation: NEW HALL

Founder: Assoc. for Women in Cambridge

Location: Huntingdon Road *(DE2)*

Date: 1958

Foundation: CHURCHILL COLLEGE

Founder: by Committee (aft. Sir Winston)

Location: Storey's Way *(CD2-3)*

Date: 1965

Foundation: DARWIN COLLEGE

Founders: Gonville & Caius, St John's & Trinity

Location: Silver Street *(F6-7)*

Date: 1965

Foundation: CLARE HALL

Founders: Clare College & Benefactors

Location: Herschel Road *(D5)*

Date: 1965: **1973**

Foundation: WOLFSON COLLEGE

Founder: The Wolfson Foundation

Location: Barton Road *(CD8)*

Date: 1974

Foundation: ROBINSON COLLEGE

Founder: Mr David Robinson

Location: Grange Road *(D5)*

Theological Colleges

Date: 1877

Foundation: RIDLEY HALL

Denomination: Church of England

Location: Ridley Hall Road *(EF7)*

Date: 1881

Foundation: WESTCOTT HOUSE

Denomination: Church of England

Location: Jesus Lane *(H4)*

Date: 1921

Foundation: WESLEY HOUSE

Denomination: Methodist

Location: Jesus Lane *(GH3-4)*

Notes: *Multiple dates refer to earlier foundations.*

Italic references in parentheses relate to the town map on page 18.

SELECT BIBLIOGRAPHY

Babington, Charles Cardale, *Ancient Cambridgeshire*, Cambridge Antiquarian Society, 1883

Black, M.H., *Cambridge University Press, 1584–1984*, Cambridge University Press, 1984

Booth, Philip and Nicholas Taylor, *Cambridge New Architecture*, London, Leonard Hill, 1970

Brooke, Christopher (ed.), *A History of the University of Cambridge*, 4 vols, Cambridge University Press, 1988–2004

Colvin, Howard, *A Biographical Dictionary of British Architects 1600–1840*, London, John Murray, 1978 (first published 1954)

Combe, William, *A History of the University of Cambridge, Its Colleges, Halls and Public Buildings*, 2 vols, published by Rudolph Ackermann, London, 1815, now abridged as *Ackermann's Cambridge* (Reginald Ross Williamson, ed.), Harmondsworth, King Penguin, 1952

Gray, Arthur, *The Town of Cambridge, a History*, Cambridge, W. Heffer, 1925

Haigh, Christopher (ed.), *Cambridge Historical Encyclopedia of Great Britain and Ireland*, Cambridge University Press, 1985

Harraden, Richard, *Cantabrigia Depicta*, Cambridge and London, Harraden & Son, 1809

Keynes, Geoffrey (ed.), *The Letters of Rupert Brooke*, London, Faber & Faber, 1968

Liscombe, R.W., *William Wilkins 1778–1839*, Cambridge University Press, 1980

Loggan, David, *Cantabrigia Illustrata*, Cambridge, 1690

Pevsner, Nikolaus, *Cambridgeshire*, Harmondsworth, Penguin Books, 1970

Rawle, Tim, *Cambridge Architecture*, London, Trefoil, 1985, André Deutsch, 1993

Roach, J.P.C. (ed.), *A History of the County of Cambridge and the Isle of Ely*, Vol. III: *The City and University of Cambridge* (series within *The Victoria History of the Counties of England*), London, Oxford University Press, 1959

Roberts, David, with a set of eight drawings by Gordon Cullen, *The Town of Cambridge as It Ought to be Reformed: the Plan of Nicholas Hawksmoor Interpreted in an Essay*, Cambridge, privately printed at the University Press, 1955

'Robinson College competition', *Architects' Journal*, 20 and 27 November 1974

Royal Commission on Historical Monuments, *City of Cambridge*, 2 vols and plans, 1959

Sicca, Cinzia Maria, *Committed to Classicism: The Building of Downing College, Cambridge*, Cambridge, Downing College, 1987

Steegmann, John, *Cambridge*, 3rd edn, London, Batsford, 1945

Trevelyan, G.M., *History of England*, The Illustrated Edition, Harlow, Longman, 1973

Watkin, David, *The Triumph of the Classical: Cambridge Architecture 1804–1834*, Cambridge University Press, 1977

Willis, Robert, edited and updated by John Willis Clark, *Architectural History of the University of Cambridge and of the Colleges of Cambridge and Eton*, 3 vols and plans, University Press, Cambridge, 1886, reprinted with new introduction by David Watkin, but without the plans, Cambridge University Press, 1988

INDEX